delicious. **5** OF THE BEST

Quadrille

5 OF THE BEST

BY VALLI LITTLE

delicious.

CELEBRATING FIVE YEARS OF THE WORLD'S BEST FOOD MAGAZINE

First published in 2006 by Quadrille Publishing Limited
Alhambra House, 27-31 Charing Cross Road, London WC2H 0LS

Reprinted in 2007
10 9 8 7 6 5 4 3 2

Text © 2006 The contributors
Photographs © 2006 The photographers
Design and layout copyright © 2006 Quadrille Publishing Ltd

Editorial director Jane O'Shea
Creative director Helen Lewis
Designer Claire Peters
Project editor Jamie Ambrose
Production Bridget Fish

Cataloguing in Publication Data: a catalogue record for this book is
available from the British Library.

ISBN 978 184400 445 4
Printed and bound in China

Welcome to the very best of delicious. The magazine began life five years ago in Australia and went from strength to strength until, in 2004, a British **delicious.** was launched. It hit the newsstands to huge acclaim and is now the biggest selling glossy food magazine in the UK. Sister publications are planned for America and Holland. You certainly can't keep a good magazine down! Right from the start it was apparent that we were on to something special. We created **delicious.** for people who love food and love to cook. We realised that you care about what's in season and what isn't and that you wanted to know the provenance of the food you put on the table. You told us that a big part of your affection for the magazine was the way it looks - superb photography in a beautifully designed package.

Here we've brought together five of the best recipes from our favourite features collected throughout the years. We know you'll

Our recipes are **easy**, **exciting** and, of course, always **delicious**!

like them as much as we do. The very best starters - hot and cold; the most delectable dishes using meat as the main ingredient; fish has a starring role and, of course, vegetables both as an accompaniment and as a main course. **delicious.** is known for its 'wicked' section and *5 of the Best* brings you a very tempting range of puddings, cakes and desserts. Our recipes are easy, exciting and, of course, always *delicious*! So whether you want a simple but scrumptious midweek meal or a special recipe for a dinner party, you'll find something to suit any occasion. And because they are delicious. recipes, you can rest assured that they'll work the first time and you won't have to search high and low to find the ingredients. Our philosophy has always been to inspire, but to keep things real. A big thank you to all our readers who have supported us right from the very start - this book is dedicated to you. Happy cooking to you all.

5 OF THE BEST
cold starters

prosciutto wraps

24 baby green beans, tops trimmed
120g micro salad leaves*
  or wild rocket
2 heaped tbsp toasted pine nuts
2 heaped tbsp freshly grated parmesan
20ml extra-virgin olive oil
juice of 1 lemon
12 thin prosciutto slices

for the dressing
20ml balsamic vinegar
60ml extra-virgin olive oil
pinch of dried chilli flakes
$1/2$ tsp chopped fresh garlic
1 heaped tbsp chopped flat-leaf parsley

Put the dressing ingredients in a small bowl, whisk with a fork and set aside.

Place the beans in a bowl, cover with boiling water and leave for 1 minute. Drain and refresh under cold water.

Combine the beans with the leaves, pine nuts and Parmesan. Drizzle with the oil and lemon juice, then season to taste. Lay out the prosciutto slices, put a handful of bean mixture on each, then roll them up. Drizzle with the dressing just before serving.

*Micro salad leaves, the first real leaves from each plant, can be found in farmers' markets and selected greengrocers.

Serves 6

simple **antipasto**

1 buffalo mozzarella (about 70g) or
  2 bocconcini, broken into pieces*
4 slices prosciutto
8 slices mild salami
2 heaped tbsp pesto
60ml extra-virgin olive oil
1 x 400g can cannellini beans, rinsed, drained
8 cooked king prawns, peeled,
  de-veined, tails intact
12 small vine-ripened tomatoes, roasted
grissini (breadsticks), to serve

Divide the cheese, prosciutto and salami among four serving plates.

Mix the pesto with the oil, then toss 1 heaped tablespoon of the pesto mixture with the beans. Add this to the plates along with the prawns and tomatoes.

Drizzle with the remaining pesto. Serve with the grissini.

*Bocconcini are small balls of mozzarella

Serves 4

sushi timbales

Timbale is a French term for a mixture prepared in a small, round mould.

½ cucumber, peeled
150ml rice vinegar
75g caster sugar
2 tsp salt
200g sushi rice
18 large smoked salmon slices
2-3 tsp wasabi paste
6 small cooked prawns, peeled
10g (or to taste) coriander
  leaves, plus extra to garnish

Oil six 100ml ramekins and line with plastic wrap.

Use a swivel peeler to shave long strips from the cucumber, turning as you go. Discard the seeds in the centre. Place the vinegar, sugar and salt in a small pan over medium heat, and stir for 1-2 minutes until the sugar is dissolved. Cool, then add 80ml of the vinegar/sugar dressing to the cucumber and refrigerate.

Place the rice in a pan with 300ml water. Bring to the boil, cover, reduce heat to low and simmer for 15 minutes. Turn off the heat and let stand for 10 minutes. Spread on a non-metallic tray or platter, sprinkle with half the remaining dressing and cool.

Line each ramekin with three salmon slices, leaving some hanging over the sides. Half-fill the moulds with cooled rice, then add a dab of wasabi and a prawn. Cover with the remaining rice. Fold in any overhanging salmon. Cover and chill for 15 minutes.

Whiz the remaining dressing in a blender with wasabi to taste and coriander.

To serve, invert the timbales onto a plate and discard the wrap. Top with cucumber and extra coriander. Drizzle with the sauce.

Serves 6

tuna-stuffed **peppers**

2 large red peppers, halved,
    seeds and membrane removed
20ml olive oil
1 x 425g can tuna in oil, drained
2 hard-boiled eggs, chopped
1 heaped tbsp capers, chopped
2 heaped tbsp chopped chives
6 tbsp good-quality mayonnaise
200g mixed salad leaves
80ml good-quality french dressing

Preheat the oven to 180°C/350°F/gas mark 4.

Place the peppers on a baking tray, cut-side up, drizzle with the oil and roast for 15 minutes. Remove and cool.

To make the filling, place the tuna, egg, capers and half the chives in a bowl. Add enough mayonnaise to bind, and season with salt and pepper.

When the peppers are cool, fill the cavities with the tuna mixture.

Toss the salad leaves with half the dressing and place on serving plates, along with the peppers. Drizzle with the remaining dressing, and garnish with the remaining chives. Season with salt and pepper to taste.

Serves 4

tuna sashimi

500g sashimi-grade tuna*
2 avocados, flesh cut into thick slices
40ml extra-virgin olive oil
20ml lime juice, plus extra lime to serve
4 spring onions, finely sliced on
    the diagonal
sea salt and black pepper
125ml light soy sauce

Using a sharp knife, cut the tuna into 0.5cm slices. Place on a serving platter with the slices of avocado.

Combine the extra-virgin olive oil and the lime juice. When ready to serve, dress the avocado and tuna with the lime dressing.

Garnish with spring onions and season with the sea salt and black pepper. Serve with the soy sauce for dipping, and extra lime, if desired.

* Sashimi grade means that the tuna must be very fresh in order to be sliced thinly.

Serves 4

5 OF THE BEST
chilled soups

herb garden soup

30g unsalted butter
3 leeks, white part only, chopped
1 garlic clove, crushed
500g potatoes, peeled and chopped
600ml chicken stock
300ml single cream
1 heaped tbsp flat-leaf parsley,
    finely chopped
1 heaped tbsp fresh chives, finely chopped
1 heaped tbsp fresh tarragon,
    finely chopped
edible flowers (such as nasturtiums,
    chive flowers or marigolds), to garnish

Melt the butter in a large saucepan over a low heat. Add the leeks and cook for 5-6 minutes or until softened, then add the garlic and cook for a further minute.

Add the potatoes and stock, increase the heat to high and bring to the boil. Reduce heat to low and simmer for 20 minutes or until the vegetables are soft.

Allow to cool slightly, then blend in batches, and season with salt and pepper. Refrigerate overnight.

Just before serving, add the cream and herbs, then stir to combine and taste for seasoning. Garnish with the edible flowers.

Serves 8-10

cucumber soup with garlic prawns

2½ cucumbers, peeled
300ml thick greek yoghurt
75ml crème fraîche
300ml chicken stock
2-3 drops tabasco sauce
1 tsp sea salt
2 heaped tbsp chopped fresh mint
2 heaped tbsp chopped fresh chives
2 heaped tbsp chopped fresh dill

for the garlic prawns
60ml olive oil
400g medium raw prawns, peeled, tails on
4 garlic cloves, sliced
1 small red chilli, seeded, thinly sliced
4 tbsp chopped flat-leaf parsley

Cut two cucumbers in half and scrape out and discard the seeds. Roughly chop the flesh and place in a processor with the yoghurt, crème fraîche, stock, Tabasco, salt and herbs. Process to combine.

Place in a bowl, cover and refrigerate. Use a vegetable peeler to cut long strips from the remaining cucumber half. Set aside.

To make the garlic prawns, heat the oil in a pan over a medium-high heat. Add the prawns, garlic and chilli and cook until the prawns are just cooked through. Season and toss in the parsley.

Place a pile of garlic prawns in each bowl, spoon on the soup and garnish with cucumber. Season with pepper.

Serves 4-6

tomato & harissa soup

1kg vine-ripened tomatoes, peeled
    and deseeded
2 garlic cloves
100g (about 5 slices) white bread,
    crusts removed
2 tsp harissa*
1 heaped tbsp tomato paste
200ml extra-virgin olive oil
2 tbsp plus 2 tsp sherry vinegar
pinch of caster sugar
natural yoghurt, paprika and
    coriander leaves, to serve

Place the tomatoes in a blender along with the garlic,
bread, harissa and tomato paste. Season and blend until
smooth, then slowly add the oil while motor is running.

Place the mixture in a bowl, stir in the vinegar and sugar,
then season again to taste. Add some warm water if it's
too thick.

Serve in glasses, with a dollop of yoghurt, paprika and
coriander leaves.

*A Tunisian chilli paste, available from selected supermarkets and
gourmet food shops.

Serves 6-8

summer **pea** soup with **smoked-trout** salad

60ml extra-virgin olive oil
1 leek, white part only, thinly sliced
400g fresh or frozen peas
1 potato, peeled, chopped
700ml chicken or vegetable stock
pinch of nutmeg
200g smoked trout
60g watercress leaves
1 small avocado, peeled, sliced
40ml lemon juice
1 baby cos lettuce, outer leaves discarded
250ml double cream

Heat 20ml of the oil in a medium saucepan over low heat, then add the leek and cook for 2-3 minutes or until just softened.

Add the peas, potato and stock, bring to the boil, then simmer for 10 minutes over a low heat. Season with salt, pepper and nutmeg. Allow to cool, place in a blender and blend until smooth, then refrigerate for 2 hours.

Remove the skin from the trout, break the flesh into large flakes and discard the skin and bones. Mix the trout with the watercress leaves and avocado, dress with the remaining olive oil and the lemon juice. Season with salt and pepper.

Place a lettuce leaf on each serving plate and fill the cavities evenly with the trout mixture. Stir the cream into the soup and taste for seasoning.

Serve with a grind of black pepper and the salad on the side.

Serves 4

salmorejo

Salmorejo is a thicker version of gazpacho – cold tomato soup – and is traditionally served in small terracotta bowls and garnished with chopped *jamón** and boiled egg.

200g (about 10 slices) sliced white
    bread, crusts removed
1kg fresh tomatoes, peeled,
    deseeded and chopped
4 garlic cloves, chopped
40ml white-wine vinegar
160ml Spanish olive oil
extra-virgin olive oil, to drizzle
shredded *jamón** and peeled,
    chopped hard-boiled egg, to serve

Place the bread in a bowl and add enough cold water to cover. Set aside for 5 minutes to soak.

Use your hands to squeeze excess water from the bread, then place in a food processor with the tomatoes, garlic, vinegar and 1 teaspoon salt. Process to combine. With the motor running, gradually add the olive oil in a thin, steady stream until well-combined.

When ready to serve, spoon the soup into small bowls, drizzle with the extra-virgin olive oil and top with the *jamón* and egg. Serve as a first course or as a cold sauce with roasted or steamed vegetables or grilled fish.

**Jamón* is Spanish ham, available from Spanish food stores and some delicatessens. If not available, substitute with good-quality cured ham.

Serves 4-6

5 OF THE BEST
hot soups

thai-style **pumpkin** soup with coriander pesto

2 bunches fresh coriander, roots trimmed
  (a few leaves reserved for garnish)
zest and juice of 1 lemon
2 garlic cloves
80ml olive oil
1 onion, chopped
2 tsp grated ginger
1 heaped tbsp thai red curry paste
1kg pumpkin, peeled, cut into small cubes
500ml vegetable stock
400ml canned light coconut milk
thinly sliced red onion and thinly sliced
  red chilli, to garnish

To make the coriander pesto, whiz the coriander, lemon zest, lemon juice and garlic in a food processor. Slowly add 60ml of the oil to make a sauce consistency, adding a little warm water if necessary, then season to taste.

Heat the remaining oil in a large pan over a medium heat. Add the onion and stir for 1 minute. Add the ginger and curry paste and stir for 1 minute.

Add the pumpkin and stock, bring to the boil, then simmer over a low heat for 15 minutes until pumpkin is cooked. Cool slightly, then blend until smooth. Return to the pan, add the coconut milk and season, then warm through.

To serve, pour the soup into bowls and swirl in a spoonful of pesto. Garnish with the onion, chilli and reserved coriander leaves.

Serves 6

cauliflower cheese soup

700g cauliflower
450ml milk
450ml single cream
1 bay leaf
50g unsalted butter
350g chopped onion
25g plain flour
200ml vegetable stock
350g gruyère or cheddar cheese
   (or half and half)
½ tsp grated nutmeg

Chop the cauliflower into small florets, discard the outer leaves and place in a pan along with the milk, cream and bay leaf. Simmer over a low heat until tender. Strain, reserving the cauliflower and the liquid.

Wipe the pan clean, return to the heat and melt the butter. Add the onion and cook over a low heat for 5 minutes, or until just softened. Add the flour and cook for 1 minute, then add the stock and strained liquid, stirring to combine. Cook for 1-2 minutes over a low to medium heat or until slightly thickened.

Add the cauliflower and 300g of the cheese and season with salt, pepper and nutmeg. (The soup can be prepared ahead up to this stage and kept refrigerated.)

Preheat the oven to 220°C/425°F/gas mark 7.

Divide the soup among six ovenproof serving bowls and sprinkle with the remaining cheese. Place the bowls in a roasting pan, pour in enough water to come halfway up the sides of the bowls and bake for 10-15 minutes, or until the cheese is bubbling and golden.

Serves 6

pasta & fagioli

150g tubetti pasta*
  (or other small soup pasta)
40ml olive oil
1 celery stalk, finely chopped
1 carrot, finely chopped
1 small onion, finely chopped
2 garlic cloves, crushed
1 sprig rosemary
2 x 400g cans cannellini beans,
  rinsed and drained
1 x 400g can borlotti beans,
  rinsed and drained
1 x 425g can whole tomatoes,
  drained and roughly chopped
1 litre vegetable stock
50g (2 handfuls) baby spinach
lemon wedges, to serve

Cook the tubetti in a large saucepan of boiling salted water according to the packet instructions, then drain.

Meanwhile, heat the oil in a large, deep saucepan over a medium-low heat. Cook the celery, carrot and onion for about 10 minutes until softened but not browned. During the final minutes of cooking, stir in the garlic and rosemary.

Process 1 can of cannellini beans (adding a little water if needed) until puréed but still chunky. Add the puréed beans, whole beans, tomatoes, stock and 250ml water to the onion mixture.

Bring to a simmer, cover and cook for 10 minutes. Remove from the heat, stir through the pasta and spinach and season. Serve with lemon wedges.

*From selected supermarkets.

Serves 4

vietnamese **pho**

500ml beef stock
1 cinnamon stick
2 star anise
3cm piece of ginger
250g flat rice stick noodles
3 bunches bok choy, halved, trimmed
400g beef fillet or rump, trimmed,
   very thinly sliced
mint and coriander leaves, and
   sliced fresh red chilli and red
   onion, to serve

Place the stock, cinnamon, star anise and ginger in a large saucepan over a medium-high heat. Add 500ml of water. Bring to the boil, then reduce the heat to medium and simmer for 15 minutes for the flavours to infuse.

Meanwhile, place the noodles in a heatproof bowl and pour on boiling water to soften. Drain and set aside.

Strain the stock, discarding any solids, and return to the heat. When boiling, add the bok choy and cook for 2 minutes until tender.

Divide the noodles and beef among serving bowls and pour on the very hot stock and vegetables. The heat from the stock will cook the meat. Serve with mint, coriander, chilli and onion.

Serves 4

easy fish chowder

20ml olive oil
200g streaky bacon, rind removed
2 onions, finely chopped
2 celery stalks, thinly sliced
1 garlic clove, crushed
1 heaped tbsp plain flour
500ml hot milk
350g desiree potatoes, peeled,
    cut into 1cm chunks
375ml fish stock
100g canned corn kernels, drained
500g boneless white fish (such as perch
    or cod), cut into bite-size chunks
24 mussels, scrubbed, de-bearded (optional)
150ml double cream
2 tbsp chopped flat-leaf parsley, to garnish

Heat the oil in a large saucepan, add the bacon and cook over a medium heat until it starts to crisp.

Add the onion and cook until it starts to soften, then add the celery and garlic and cook for 1-2 minutes to soften. Add the flour and cook for 1 minute. Stir in the hot milk, add the potatoes and stock and cook for 5 minutes.

Stir in the corn and fish, and cook for a further 5 minutes, or until the fish is opaque. If using mussels, add these during the last 2 minutes of the fish's cooking time (discarding any that haven't opened).

Stir in the cream, and season with salt and pepper. Serve in deep bowls sprinkled with the parsley.

Serves 6

5 OF THE BEST
5 eggs

egg & chips

3 desiree potatoes, peeled, thinly sliced
40-60ml extra-virgin olive oil
20ml white-wine vinegar
4 free-range eggs
4 large lettuce leaves
8 cherry tomatoes, halved

for the dressing
20ml lemon juice
60ml extra-virgin olive oil
1 tsp sugar
1 garlic clove, bruised

Preheat the oven to 180°C/350°F/gas mark 4.

Stack the potato slices into 12 piles and place on a baking tray lined with baking paper. Drizzle each stack with a little oil and season with salt. Bake for 30-35 minutes, or until cooked.

Fill a shallow saucepan with water, bring to a simmer, then add the vinegar. Make a whirlpool using a spoon and crack in the first egg, then the second. Cook for 3 minutes, or until the egg white is just set. Remove the eggs with a slotted spoon, and cover with foil to keep warm while you repeat this process for the remaining eggs.

To make the dressing, whisk together all the ingredients until combined.

To serve, place a lettuce leaf on each plate. Top with potato, tomato and a poached egg, then drizzle with the dressing.

Serves 4

coddled eggs with crunchy croûtons & smoked salmon

150g cubed firm white bread
30ml olive oil
6 tbsp chopped fresh herbs,
   (such as chives,
   parsley and thyme)
150g baby spinach leaves
6 large free-range eggs
250ml double cream
12 slices smoked salmon

Preheat the oven to 170°C/325°F/gas mark 3.

Toss the bread cubes with the oil and 2 tablespoons of the chopped herbs. Spread onto a baking tray and toast in oven for 8 minutes, or until crisp and golden. Set aside.

Wash the spinach and, without draining, place in a saucepan over a medium heat. Allow to wilt, remove from the pan and rinse under cold water. Squeeze to remove excess water, then season to taste.

Butter six small heatproof glasses or egg coddlers*. Divide the spinach among them, break an egg into each and drizzle with cream. Sprinkle with the remaining herbs and season with salt and pepper.

Cover each glass tightly with foil (or clip lids, if using coddlers) and place in a saucepan of simmering water so that the water comes halfway up the sides. Simmer for 6 minutes, remove from the heat and leave the glasses or coddlers to sit in the water for another 4 minutes.

Place the eggs in their dishes onto plates, and serve with the croûtons and smoked salmon.

*From selected kitchenware shops.

Serves 6

asian-style **fried egg** on bean sprout salad

250g bean sprouts
150g mange-tout, thinly sliced
    on the diagonal
2 spring onions, thinly sliced
    on the diagonal
1 long red chilli, thinly sliced
vegetable oil, for frying
4 eggs

for the dressing
50ml rice vinegar
20ml reduced-salt soy sauce
1 heaped tbsp caster sugar
1 tsp sesame oil

To make the dressing, whisk together all the ingredients in a small bowl.

Put the bean sprouts, mange-tout, spring onion and chilli in a large bowl. Add the dressing, then toss gently to combine.

Fill a wok with about 6cm of oil and place over a high heat. When hot (almost smoking), crack an egg into the oil. Fry about 30 seconds each side, turning with a slotted spoon, or until the egg is golden and puffed. Remove and drain on paper towels. Repeat with the remaining eggs.

Divide the salad among serving plates, reserving a little for garnish. Top each plate with an egg and garnish with reserved salad.

Serves 4

the **perfect** herb omelette

3 fresh free-range eggs
sea salt and freshly ground
  black pepper
1 tsp unsalted butter
½ tsp extra-virgin olive oil
2½ tbsp chopped fresh herbs
  such as chives, parsley,
  basil and marjoram
bread, to serve

Place the eggs in a bowl and whisk lightly to combine.
Season with sea salt and black pepper.

Put the butter and oil in an omelette or small frying pan over
a medium-high heat (the oil prevents the butter from burning
as the pan needs to be quite hot). When the butter starts to
froth, add the egg mixture and, as the base begins to cook,
use a fork to draw it aside and allow the uncooked egg to
run beneath.

Continue doing this until the omelette is set but still soft.

Scatter the herbs on top, fold over one side of the omelette
and carefully ease onto a plate. Serve with a glass of wine
and some good bread.

Serves 1

spiced **coconut** eggs

100g unsalted butter
2 onions, thinly sliced
3 tsp good-quality mild curry powder
6-8 fresh curry leaves*
200ml hollandaise sauce*
200ml coconut cream
200ml double cream
100ml vegetable stock or water
40ml lemon juice
8 hard-boiled eggs, peeled
4 spring onions, sliced on the diagonal
steamed basmati rice and poppadams,
   to serve
toasted shaved coconut and paprika,
   to garnish

Place the butter in a saucepan, add the onions and cook over a low heat, stirring, for 6-8 minutes until softened but not coloured.

Add the curry powder and leaves and cook for a further minute. Stir in the hollandaise, coconut cream, double cream, stock and lemon juice.

Add the eggs to warm through, along with half of the onion.

Serve with rice and/or poppadams, and garnish with coconut, the remaining onion and paprika.

*Curry leaves are from greengrocers. Hollandaise sauce is available from supermarkets and delis.

Serves 4

5 OF THE BEST
boiled pasta

pasta **puttanesca**

40ml olive oil
2 garlic cloves, chopped
1 small red chilli, finely chopped
75g pitted green olives, sliced
75g pitted black olives, sliced
6 semi-dried tomatoes, cut into thin strips
2$\frac{1}{2}$ tbsp salted capers, rinsed
1 x 425g can chopped tomatoes
400g spaghetti
40g fresh basil leaves, shredded
grated parmesan, to serve

Heat the oil in a frying pan. Add the garlic and chilli and cook over a medium heat for 1 minute.

Add the olives, semi-dried tomatoes, capers and diced tomatoes and simmer for 20 minutes. Season with pepper to taste.

Cook the pasta according to the packet directions. Drain and return to the pan. Add the sauce and basil and toss together.

Serve sprinkled with Parmesan.

Serves 4

pasta with lemon & goat cheese

400g spiral pasta
40ml olive oil
3 garlic cloves, crushed
¼ tsp dried chilli flakes
grated zest of 2 lemons
80ml lemon juice
300g matured goat cheese*
100g wild rocket
4 tbsp grated parmesan

Cook the pasta according to the packet instructions in a large pan of boiling salted water until *al dente*.

Meanwhile, heat the oil in a deep frying pan over a medium heat. Add the garlic and stir for 30 seconds. Add the chilli, lemon zest and juice. Drain the pasta and add to the frying pan along with 125ml of the cooking water. Toss, remove from the heat and cover.

Heat the grill to high. Cut the cheese into four rounds, place them on a lightly greased baking tray and grill for 2-3 minutes, until bubbling.

Toss the Parmesan and rocket with the pasta and season.

To serve, divide the pasta among four bowls and top each with a slice of grilled goat cheese and freshly ground black pepper.

*Or crumble fresh goat cheese over the finished pasta.

Serves 4

pasta with **pepper steak**

400g tagliatelle
80ml olive oil
50g unsalted butter
450g rump steak, trimmed
½ onion, halved, thinly sliced
1 heaped tbsp green peppercorns
   in brine
2 garlic cloves, finely chopped
200g button mushrooms,
   thinly sliced
200ml dry white wine
2 tsp dijon mustard
20ml worcestershire sauce
125ml beef stock
125ml double cream
2 heaped tbsp flat-leaf
   parsley, chopped

Cook the pasta according to the packet instructions, then drain. Toss with 20ml of the olive oil, season with salt and pepper to taste and set aside.

Heat the butter and the remaining oil in a large frying pan over a very high heat, add the steak and cook for 1-2 minutes each side; remove and set aside. Reduce the heat to medium, add the onion and cook, stirring occasionally, for 4-5 minutes until soft. Add the drained peppercorns, garlic, mushrooms and wine and cook for a further 2-3 minutes.

Add the mustard, Worcestershire sauce, stock and cream, season well, then allow to simmer for 2 minutes.

Slice the steak thinly and add to the pan with the pasta and parsley, then toss gently to combine.

Serves 4

spaghetti with **ricotta & rocket**

200g rocket
100ml extra-virgin olive oil
3 garlic cloves, crushed
2 red chillies, seeds removed,
  finely chopped
60g fresh basil leaves
200g low-fat ricotta cheese
400g spaghetti
100g grated parmesan

Roughly chop half the rocket.

Heat 40ml of the oil in a frying pan over a medium heat, add the garlic and chilli and fry for 1 minute.

Add the basil and chopped rocket and cook for 2-3 minutes or until wilted. Place in a food processor along with the ricotta, the remaining oil and half the remaining rocket, and process to combine. Season well.

Cook the pasta in a large pot of boiling, salted water until *al dente*. Drain, and add sauce, remaining rocket and half the Parmesan, then toss to combine.

Serve topped with the remaining Parmesan.

Serves 4

bucatini with
salsa verde

8 anchovy fillets
2 garlic cloves, crushed
2 heaped tbsp small salted capers,
    rinsed and drained
40ml smooth mustard
juice of 1 lemon
1 heaped tbsp thinly sliced lemon zest
80ml extra-virgin olive oil
4 vine-ripened tomatoes, peeled,
    deseeded and chopped
60g pitted green olives, chopped
40g pitted kalamata
    olives, chopped
375g bucatini or pappardelle pasta
60g fresh flat-leaf parsley
80g firmly packed fresh basil leaves

Place the anchovy fillets and garlic on a chopping board and use a mezzaluna* or sharp knife to finely chop until you have a paste. Put in a bowl and add the capers, mustard and lemon juice and zest. Stir to combine. Gradually whisk in the oil until it forms a thick emulsion. Stir in the tomatoes and olives.

Bring a large saucepan of salted water to the boil, add the pasta and cook until *al dente*. Drain and return to the saucepan while you finish the sauce.

Roughly chop the parsley and basil leaves and stir into the sauce. Ladle the sauce into the pasta and toss to combine.

Serve immediately.

* A mezzaluna is an Italian chopping implement – much favoured by Nigella Lawson, incidentally. As its name suggests, it is half-moon shaped with handles at both ends. Use a rocking action to chop. Available at kitchenware shops.

Serves 4

5 OF THE BEST
baked pasta

turkey macaroni bake

75g unsalted butter, plus extra
   knobs to bake
50g plain flour
850ml turkey or chicken stock
1/2 tsp grated nutmeg
300ml double cream
2 tsp lemon zest
150g dried macaroni
10ml olive oil
200g sliced portobello mushrooms
120g (approximately) baby spinach
   (optional)
60ml dry marsala or white wine
juice of 1/2 lemon
700g cooked turkey meat, diced
2 tsp fresh thyme, chopped
50g flaked almonds, roasted
50g grated parmesan

Preheat the oven to 180°C/350°F/gas mark 4.

Melt 50g of butter in a saucepan over low heat, then add the flour and cook for two minutes, stirring, to prevent it from catching. Whisk in the stock. Bring to the boil, then reduce the heat and cook for five minutes, stirring. Add the nutmeg, cream and lemon zest and season well. Simmer for five minutes.

Meanwhile, cook the pasta in a pan of boiling salted water following the packet directions. Drain and refresh. Stir through the oil to prevent it from sticking.

Heat the remaining butter in a pan over a medium heat. When it is sizzling, add the mushrooms and cook, stirring, for 1-2 minutes. (Add the washed baby spinach during the last minute of cooking the mushrooms, if desired.) Add the marsala and lemon juice and cook for a further minute.

Combine the sauce, turkey, thyme, pasta, mushrooms and cooking juices in a bowl. Transfer into a 2-litre baking dish and sprinkle with the almonds, Parmesan and extra butter. Bake for 30 minutes, then serve.

Serves 4–6

butternut &
goat cheese lasagne

1kg butternut squash, peeled,
    cut into 4cm pieces
80ml olive oil
2 sprigs fresh rosemary
    (leaves only)
30g unsalted butter
2 leeks, thinly sliced, washed
300g baby spinach leaves,
    washed, dried
2 garlic cloves, crushed
400ml good-quality passata
3 (23cm x 15cm) sheets
    fresh lasagne
150g soft goat cheese, crumbled
40g freshly grated parmesan

Preheat the oven to 200°C/400°F/gas mark 6.

Place the squash in a roasting pan and toss in 40ml of the olive oil. Chop half the rosemary leaves, sprinkle over the pumpkin and season with salt and pepper. Roast for 30 minutes or until tender. Transfer to a bowl, mash and set aside to cool.

Heat the remaining oil and butter in a medium frying pan over low heat, add the leeks and cook, stirring, for about 5-6 minutes, or until softened. Add the spinach and garlic, and cook for a further 1-2 minutes or until the spinach is wilted. Set aside to cool.

Grease a 23cm x 15cm ovenproof dish. Spoon 80ml of the tomato passata into the base of the dish and season with salt and pepper. Place a sheet of lasagne on top and spread with mashed squash. Add another layer of lasagne, pressing down on top, then 80ml of passata, then a layer of leek and spinach. Finally, add another layer of lasagne and spread it with the remaining tomato passata.

Mix together the goat cheese, Parmesan and remaining rosemary and sprinkle over the top. Cover with foil and bake for 30 minutes, then remove the foil and return to the oven for a further 15 minutes, or until the top is golden. Remove from the oven and set aside for 5 minutes before cutting.

Note: You can use the precooked dry lasagne sheets, but you may need to increase the cooking time by a further 15 minutes. The lasagne may be assembled a few hours before cooking; alternatively, cook it the day before, refrigerate overnight, then cover with foil and reheat in a 180°C/350°F/gas mark 4 oven for 30 minutes.

Serves 6

pasta **stacks**

This is inspired by a recipe by Australian chef Belinda Jeffery.

1kg butternut squash,
    peeled, cut into small chunks
70ml olive oil, plus extra
    to serve
2 red peppers
2 yellow pepper
1kg small vine-ripened cherry
    tomatoes, 6 with stems intact
1 garlic clove, cut into slivers
18 (10 x 6cm) fresh green
    lasagne sheets
800g low-fat ricotta cheese
40g basil leaves, chopped
15g lemon thyme
    leaves, chopped
2 heaped tbsp flat-leaf
    parsley, chopped
5 tbsp grated parmesan
olive oil and balsamic vinegar,
    to serve

Preheat the oven to 190°C/375°F/gas mark 5.

Toss the squash in 40ml of the olive oil, season with salt and pepper and place on a large baking tray. Roast for 25 minutes, or until soft and lightly golden. At the same time, roast the pepper for 15 minutes, or until skin is charred, then remove from the oven and place in a plastic bag. Set aside until cooled completely, then remove and discard the charred skin, seeds and core. Cut the pepper into 3cm-wide strips.

Mash the squash and set aside.

Place the tomatoes on a roasting tray, drizzle with 20ml of the olive oil and scatter the garlic slivers over the top. Roast for 8 minutes, or until slightly wilted. Reserve the 6 tomatoes with stems for garnish and place the remaining tomatoes in a bowl. Roughly mash with a fork, then season with salt, pepper and a pinch of sugar.

Place the lasagne sheets in a large pan of boiling, salted water and cook for 2-3 minutes or until al dente. Transfer to a bowl of cold water to stop lasagne cooking, then drain on a tea towel.

Combine the ricotta, fresh herbs and half the Parmesan in a bowl, and season with salt and pepper.

To assemble, place a sheet of baking paper on a large baking tray. Place 6 sheets of lasagne on the tray. Layer the squash on top, followed by half of the ricotta mixture, then the tomatoes. Add another layer of lasagne, followed by the roasted pepper, then the remaining ricotta and finally a layer of lasagne.

Brush the tops of the lasagne sheets with 2 teaspoons of olive oil and sprinkle with the remaining Parmesan. Cover the whole tray loosely with foil, place in the oven and heat for 10 minutes. The lasagne should be eaten warm, not hot. Use a fish slice to place each lasagne on a serving plate, drizzle with a little oil and balsamic, and serve with the reserved tomatoes.

Serves 6

lamb & pasta bake with roasted tomatoes

1.2kg diced lamb (shoulder or leg)
2 onions, thinly sliced
juice of 1 small lemon
60ml olive oil, plus extra to drizzle
3 tsp dried oregano
2 tsp ground cumin
2 tsp sweet smoked
  paprika (*pimentón**)
1 litre chicken or beef stock
2 heaped tbsp tomato paste
400g canned chopped tomatoes
400g orzo* pasta (or risoni)
24 cherry tomatoes on the vine
2 heaped tbsp chopped
  flat-leaf parsley
250ml thick greek yoghurt

Preheat the oven to 180°C/350°F/gas mark 4.

Place the lamb in a single layer in a large baking dish, cover with the onions and drizzle with the lemon juice and the oil. Sprinkle with the oregano, cumin and paprika, and season to taste. Toss, cover and roast for 40 minutes, stirring occasionally.

Heat the stock in a pan over medium heat and whisk in the tomato paste. Remove the lamb from the oven, pour in the stock, add the canned tomatoes, cover with foil and return to the oven for 1 hour. Remove, sprinkle in the pasta, cover and return to the oven for 20 minutes, until the pasta is cooked and most liquid absorbed. Put the cherry tomatoes on a baking tray, drizzle with olive oil, season and roast for final 5 minutes of the lamb's cooking time. To serve, stir through the parsley, divide among bowls, and top with the yoghurt and a few tomatoes.

Pimentón is available from spice shops and selected delis. Orzo (or risoni) is rice-shaped pasta available from supermarkets.

Serves 8

baked penne with **roasted vegetables**

2 spanish onions, cut into wedges

2 leeks, sliced

2 courgettes, cut into chunks

1 fennel bulb, cut into wedges

250g punnet red cherry tomatoes

250g punnet yellow
  cherry tomatoes

1 sweet potato, peeled,
  cut into chunks

2 heaped tbsp chopped
  fresh thyme

120ml olive oil

350g penne pasta

6 anchovies

6 (100g) thin slices prosciutto

1 garlic clove

60g torn fresh basil leaves

200g bocconcini (*see* p. 11),
  cut into small chunks

80ml single cream

Preheat oven to 200°C/400°F/gas mark 6.

Put all vegetables and the tomatoes on a large baking tray, sprinkle with the thyme and drizzle with 40ml of the olive oil. Toss well. Season with salt and freshly ground black pepper and roast in the preheated oven for 30 minutes.

Cook the penne in a large saucepan of boiling salted water following the packet directions, or until *al dente*. Place the anchovies, prosciutto, garlic and basil in a food processor. Add the remaining olive oil and process until it resembles a coarse paste.

In a large saucepan, toss together the roasted vegetables and their cooking juices, the anchovy paste and the pasta. Stir in the bocconcini and cream, then pour into a large baking dish. Bake in the oven for 15 minutes.

Serve the baked penne straight from the baking dish.

Serves 6

5 OF THE BEST
pizzas

bread pizzas

4 small ciabattas or ficelle
olive oil, to brush, plus extra to drizzle
2 garlic cloves, crushed
300g jar puttanesca or arrabbiata
  pasta sauce (or *see* recipe, p. 41)
60g black olives, pitted
2 heaped tbsp baby capers
1 red pepper, seeded, roasted, sliced
8 anchovy fillets, optional
125g grated mozzarella cheese
chopped basil, to garnish

Preheat the oven to 200°C/400°F/gas mark 6.

Cut the bread in half through the middle, then half again lengthways so you have 4 pieces. Brush the outer crust with olive oil.

Stir the garlic into the puttanesca sauce.

Place the bread halves on a baking sheet, cut-side up, and spread with the sauce. Sprinkle with the olives and capers, top with the pepper and season with pepper. Lay the anchovy fillets across the top, sprinkle with the mozzarella and bake for 15 minutes, until crisp and golden.

Drizzle with extra olive oil and garnish with basil. Serve with a green salad.

Serves 4

deli pizza

2 x 335g fresh pizza bases
250ml tomato pasta sauce
1 roasted pepper, thinly sliced
3 thin slices chargrilled aubergine*, halved
2-3 bocconcini (*see* p. 11), thinly sliced
50g prosciutto (about 3 thin slices),
    halved widthways
50g thinly sliced pepperoni
extra-virgin olive oil, to serve
3-4 tbsp fresh oregano leaves

Preheat the oven to 240°C/475°F/gas mark 9.

Cook the pizza bases on an oiled baking sheet for about 3 minutes, until the edges begin to brown and turn crisp.

Spread each pizza base with tomato pasta sauce and divide the remaining ingredients (except oregano leaves) between them, finishing with the prosciutto and pepperoni so that they crisp up a little in the oven.

Cook the pizzas for 5 minutes, or until the cheese is melted and the crust is crisp. Remove from the oven, drizzle with a little extra-virgin olive oil and scatter with oregano leaves.

* Ready-made roasted pepper and chargrilled aubergine are available from some supermarkets and delis.

Serves 4

potato pizza

1 tsp honey
7g dried yeast
375g strong bread flour,
   plus extra to knead
80ml olive oil, plus extra
   to grease
2 tsp polenta
6 garlic cloves, skin on,
   lightly crushed
2 heaped tbsp chopped mixed
   herbs (such as rosemary
   and thyme)
450g red-skinned potatoes,
   thinly sliced

Preheat the oven to 200°C/400°F/gas mark 6.

Place the honey and 250ml warm water in a bowl, and stir to combine. Sprinkle with the yeast. Set aside for 10 minutes, by which time it should start to foam (if not, your yeast is dead and you will have to start again).

Sift the flour into a large bowl, add the yeast mixture and 20ml of the olive oil, and use your hands to bring it together to form a smooth ball. Turn onto a floured surface and knead for 10 minutes until smooth. Roll out to a 30cm circle.

Brush a pizza plate or baking tray with a little oil and sprinkle with polenta. Place the dough on the tray. Place the garlic, herbs and remaining oil in a bowl and brush a little over the pizza base. Arrange the potato, overlapping, on top, then brush with more oil. Scatter the garlic over the pizza and bake for 35-40 minutes, or until golden. Drizzle with any remaining oil.

Serves 4-6

wild-mushroom pizza

30ml olive oil, plus extra
   to drizzle
2 garlic cloves, crushed
250g mixed wild mushrooms such as
   shiitake and oyster, sliced if large
250g portobello mushrooms, sliced
100g baby spinach leaves
½ lemon, juiced
2 (15cm each) bought pizza bases
125g soft goat cheese
2 heaped tbsp chopped fresh chives
crème fraîche (optional)

Preheat the oven to 200°C/400°F/gas mark 6.

Heat the olive oil in a frying pan over high heat. When it is very hot, add the garlic and mushrooms and cook quickly, until the mushrooms are just wilted but not releasing any liquid. Add the spinach and lemon juice and allow spinach to just wilt. Season with salt and cracked black pepper, then remove from heat.

Spread the pizza bases with the goat cheese and place them on a baking tray.

Pile the mushroom mixture on top and drizzle with a little more oil. Bake in the oven for 10 minutes. Sprinkle with chives to serve and a dollop of crème fraîche, if desired.

Serves 3–4

midweek pizza

1 x 280g jar artichoke hearts marinated in olive oil, quartered
2 (about 100g each) individual pizza bases or naan bread
175g taleggio cheese*, sliced
200g pimento-stuffed green olives
2 tsp thyme leaves
2 heaped tbsp grated parmesan
1 heaped tbsp flat-leaf parsley, roughly chopped

Preheat the oven to 200°C/400°F/gas mark 6.

Drain the artichokes and reserve the oil.

Place the pizza bases on a baking tray, dividing the taleggio between them. Top with the artichokes, olives and thyme, then sprinkle with the Parmesan, sea salt and black pepper.

Drizzle with a little reserved artichoke oil and bake for 10 minutes, or until the cheese is bubbling. Sprinkle with parsley before serving.

*Available from good delicatessens.

Serves 2

5 OF THE BEST
savoury tarts

little **hummus** & **herb salad** tarts

125g plain flour
$\frac{1}{2}$ tsp mild paprika
65g unsalted butter, chopped
1 egg, beaten
80ml extra-virgin olive oil
40ml lemon juice
100g mixed baby salad leaves
  (including herbs* and
  edible flowers)
260g good-quality hummus

Sift the flour into a bowl, add a pinch of salt and the paprika. Rub in the butter with your fingertips until the mixture resembles fine breadcrumbs. Add half the egg and mix first with a knife, then with your hands, until the mixture comes together to form a smooth ball. Wrap in plastic for 30 minutes, then roll out thinly on a lightly floured surface. Line six 9cm-diameter loose-bottomed tart pans with the pastry, then refrigerate for a further 30 minutes (chilling helps prevent shrinkage).

Preheat the oven to 180°C/350°F/gas mark 4.

Line the pastry shells with baking paper and pastry weights or uncooked rice. Bake for 10 minutes, then remove the paper and weights or rice. Brush the shells with the remaining egg. Bake for 5 minutes, or until crisp and golden.

When ready to serve, combine the oil and lemon juice and season with salt and pepper. Toss the herbs and salad leaves in the lemon dressing. Fill the shells with hummus and pile the salad on top.

*Baby herbs are available from selected greengrocers and farmers' markets.

Makes 6

fig & goat cheese tranche

1 block (375g) puff pastry
1 egg, beaten
160g good-quality
　　fig jam*
120g soft goat cheese
1 tsp chopped rosemary
3-4 ripe figs,
　　cut into wedges
20ml honey

Preheat the oven to 180°C/350°F/gas mark 4.

Line a baking sheet with baking paper.

Roll out the pastry to an 18cm x 30cm rectangle. Brush the top with egg and prick with a fork. Place on a baking sheet and bake for 10 minutes. Remove and lay another tray on top, and return to oven for 10 minutes. Remove and allow to cool slightly.

Preheat the grill to medium-high.

Spread the jam over the pastry base, crumble the cheese over that, sprinkle with the rosemary and season to taste. Lay the figs on top.

Place under the grill for 2-3 minutes until the cheese is lightly golden. Drizzle with honey. Serve with a green salad.

*Available from gourmet food stores. Use Onion Marmalade (*see* p. 69) if unavailable.

Serves 3-4

mascarpone & gorgonzola tart

4 eggs
450g mascarpone cheese
225g gorgonzola cheese

for the pastry
150g plain flour
75g wholemeal flour
125g unsalted butter,
   chilled and diced
60ml iced water

To make the pastry, place the flours in a food processor and pulse for a few seconds. Add the butter and whiz until the mixture resembles fine breadcrumbs. Pour in the water and process until the mixture forms a ball. Cover in plastic wrap and refrigerate for 30 minutes.

Roll out the pastry on a lightly floured surface and use it to line a lightly greased 28cm loose-bottomed tart pan. Refrigerate for 30 minutes (chilling helps prevent shrinkage).

Preheat the oven to 180°C/350°F/gas mark 4.

Line the tart pan with baking paper and fill with baking weights or rice. Blind bake for 10 minutes; remove the paper and weights.

Whiz the eggs and cheeses in a food processor until smooth, and then season. Pour into the tart shell and bake for 35 minutes or until golden and set. Serve with balsamic onions.

Serves 6-8

torta **caprese**

375g block puff pastry
1 egg, beaten
4 vine-ripened tomatoes
3 buffalo mozzarella, or
    4 bocconcini (*see* p. 11)
125g onion marmalade*
extra-virgin olive oil
fresh basil leaves, torn

for the onion marmalade
40ml olive oil
3 large onions, sliced
60ml verjuice*
1 tbsp brown sugar
40ml balsamic vinegar
2 heaped tbsp
    redcurrant jelly

Preheat oven to 200°C/400°F/gas mark 6.

Line a large baking tray with non-stick baking paper.

On a lightly floured surface, roll out the pastry to a 30cm x 15cm rectangle. Transfer it to a baking tray and brush with the beaten egg. Use a fork to prick the surface. Place the pastry in the fridge for 10 minutes to chill (chilling helps prevent shrinkage).

Cook the pastry on the middle shelf of the oven for 20-25 minutes until slightly risen and golden brown. The pastry can be cooked in advance and kept at room temperature until ready to serve.

Just before you are ready to serve, slice the tomatoes and mozzarella into 5mm slices.

Spread the onion marmalade over the top of the pastry; it will crumble and crack a bit. Alternate tomatoes and mozzarella in two lines over the marmalade and drizzle with the oil. Return to the oven and bake for no more than 5 minutes to heat through.

Garnish with basil and season with salt and freshly ground black pepper.

* Available from gourmet food shops or try the quick recipe below.

Onion marmalade
Heat the olive oil in a frying pan over a low heat and add the sliced onions. Cook for 10 minutes, or until soft. Increase the heat to medium and cook until the onions start to brown. Add the verjuice (or water) and the brown sugar. Cook until the liquid has been absorbed. Add the balsamic vinegar and redcurrant jelly and cook until the mixture has a soft, jam-like consistency.

* Verjuice is available from gourmet food stores.

Serves 4-6

roasted **vegetable** tart

1 small aubergine
1 red pepper, halved,
  seeds removed
2 small courgettes
1 red onion
1 small sweet potato, peeled
2 garlic cloves, crushed
100ml olive oil
1 x 375g block
  shortcrust pastry
300g low-fat ricotta cheese
2 eggs
50g grated parmesan
2 tsp chopped rosemary

Preheat the oven to 190°C/375°F/gas mark 5.

Grease a 30cm x 11cm loose-bottomed, rectangular tart pan.

Cut the aubergine, pepper, courgette, onion and sweet potato into 2cm chunks. Place in a bowl with the garlic and olive oil, and toss to coat in the oil. Tip the vegetables onto a large baking tray and spread out evenly. Bake in the oven for 20 minutes, or until cooked through and slightly charred, then set aside.

Roll out the pastry on a lightly floured surface. Line the prepared pan with the pastry, then line that with baking paper. Fill with pastry weights or rice and blind bake for 10 minutes. Remove the weights and paper.

Meanwhile, beat together the ricotta, eggs, Parmesan and rosemary. Fill the pre-baked tart shell with the ricotta mixture and place in the oven for 15 minutes, or until set. Top with roasted vegetables, then return to the oven for 5 minutes to warm through. Garnish with extra rosemary, if desired.

Serves 4

5 OF THE BEST
rice

smoked fish risotto with poached eggs

40ml white-wine vinegar
4 eggs
300ml milk
1 bay leaf
250g smoked cod
50g unsalted butter
20ml olive oil
1 large leek, white part only,
    washed, thinly sliced
2 garlic cloves, crushed
250g arborio rice
150ml white wine
350ml fish or vegetable stock
120g frozen peas
2 heaped tbsp chopped chives,
    to garnish

Bring a shallow pan of water to the boil, add the vinegar, then turn the heat down to medium-low. Break the eggs into the simmering water and poach for 5 minutes until the white is cooked through but the yolk is still soft. Remove with a slotted spoon and set aside on a plate.

Put the milk, bay leaf and fish in a saucepan and poach for 5 minutes. Drain and reserve the liquid. Break the fish into pieces, discard any skin or bones and set aside.

Melt half the butter with the oil in a heavy-based frying pan over a medium heat, add the leek and cook for 1-2 minutes, until softened but not coloured. Add the garlic and fry for a few seconds, then add the rice and stir for 1 minute. Add wine and cook until there is no liquid left.

Add half the stock, bring to the boil, then reduce the heat to low and simmer until there is no liquid left. Add the remaining stock and bring to the boil again, then turn the heat to low and cook, stirring, for another 7 minutes, until the rice is cooked.

Stir in the strained poaching liquid and peas and cook, stirring, for another 2-3 minutes. Season, then stir in the fish and the remaining butter. Remove from heat and cover.

To reheat the eggs, fill a bowl with boiling water, place each egg on a slotted spoon and drop into the water for 1 minute to heat through, then drain. To serve, divide the risotto among bowls, top with the egg, sprinkle with cracked pepper and the chopped chives.

Serves 4

nasi goreng

1 onion, peeled, roughly chopped
1 red chilli, deseeded, chopped
1 tsp shrimp paste (*blachan*)*
2 garlic cloves
2 tsp tomato paste
2 tsp *kecap manis**
60ml vegetable oil
225g long-grain rice*
2 eggs
1/2 tsp sesame oil
125g thin french beans,
    trimmed, blanched
450g cooked prawns,
    peeled, de-veined
5 spring onions, cut into
    3cm lengths
20ml light soy sauce
4 tbsp chopped fresh coriander
fried asian shallots* and sweet
    chilli sauce, to serve

Place the onion, chilli, shrimp paste, garlic, tomato paste, *kecap manis* and 20ml of the vegetable oil in a blender or processor and whiz until you have a fine paste. Set aside.

Cook the rice in salted water until just cooked. Drain, refresh under cold water, then drain well again.

Beat the eggs and season with salt and pepper. Brush the base of a non-stick frying pan with sesame oil, then add half the egg mixture and swirl to cover base. Cook over a medium heat until set, then flip over and quickly cook the other side. Repeat with the remaining egg mixture.

Stack the two omelettes on top of each other, roll together then slice thinly. Set aside.

Pour the remaining vegetable oil in a wok over a high heat. Add the paste mixture and cook for 1-2 minutes. Add the rice and stir quickly for a further 1-2 minutes. Add the beans, prawns, spring onions, soy sauce and coriander, stirring to combine until heated through. Add the omelette.

Pile the mixture onto plates, and top with fried shallots and sweet chilli sauce to serve.

*Shrimp paste, *kecap manis* (sweet soy sauce) and fried Asian shallots are available from Asian supermarkets. Leftover cooked rice works really well in this recipe; you will need 650g.

Serves 4-6

pumpkin & goat cheese risotto

20g unsalted butter
1 large leek (white part only),
    finely chopped
2 garlic cloves, crushed
500g pumpkin, peeled, diced into
    1cm pieces
zest of 1 lemon
1 heaped tbsp chopped
    thyme leaves
100ml dry white wine
900ml chicken or vegetable stock
250g arborio rice
60g frozen peas
100g soft goat cheese, crumbled
baby rocket leaves, to serve

Melt the butter in a deep frying pan over a low heat. Cook the leek for 2-3 minutes, until softened. Add the garlic, pumpkin, half the zest and half the thyme, then stir to coat. Add the wine, cover and cook for 10 minutes, or until the pumpkin is almost cooked.

Meanwhile, bring the stock to the boil in a pan. Reduce the heat to very low and simmer.

Add the rice to the pumpkin mixture and cook for 1-2 minutes to coat the grains. Add the stock 1 ladleful at a time, allowing each to be absorbed before adding the next. Continue for 12 minutes, stirring constantly, until the stock is absorbed and the rice is cooked but firm to the bite. Season to taste. Stir in the peas and half the cheese.

Serve topped with the remaining zest, thyme, cheese and rocket.

Serves 4-6

stir-fried **vegetable** rice

It's best if you cook the rice for this recipe the day before.

225g jasmine rice
1 courgette, cut into thin sticks
120g thin french beans, trimmed
1 bunch asparagus, woody ends
   trimmed, halved lengthways
60g frozen peas
1 small carrot, peeled,
   cut into thin strips
40ml vegetable oil
1 heaped tbsp green curry paste
1 small onion, chopped
2 garlic cloves, crushed
2 tsp grated fresh ginger
20ml fish sauce
20ml soy sauce
15g thai basil leaves*
6 spring onions, sliced

Cook the rice in a saucepan of boiling, salted water, then drain well. Allow to cool, then refrigerate overnight.

Blanch the courgette, beans, asparagus, peas and carrot in boiling, salted water for 1 minute, then drain, refresh under cold water and set aside.

Heat the oil in a wok over a high heat, then add the curry paste and stir-fry for a few seconds, or until fragrant. Add the onion, garlic and ginger, and cook for 1 minute. Add the blanched vegetables and cook for 2-3 minutes, or until just tender. Add the rice and heat through, then stir in the fish and soy sauces, basil leaves and spring onions.

*Thai basil is available from Asian supermarkets. Substitute with common basil if not available.

Serves 4

easy paella

20ml olive oil
500g chicken breast fillets (preferably
   with skin), cut into bite-sized pieces
1 onion, finely chopped
1 *chorizo* sausage*, chopped
200g basmati rice
1 tsp ground turmeric
425g can chopped tomatoes, drained
1 red pepper, chopped
2 garlic cloves, crushed
1 small red chilli, deseeded and
   finely chopped
500ml chicken stock
250g cooked prawns, peeled
1 x 425g can cannellini beans,
   rinsed and drained
100g baby green beans, topped,
   blanched and refreshed in cold water
2 heaped tbsp chopped coriander leaves
lemon wedges, to serve

Heat the oil in a large, deep frying pan over a medium heat. Cook the chicken pieces in batches for 3-4 minutes, turning, until golden and cooked through. Remove and set aside to drain on paper towels.

Add the onion and chorizo to the pan and cook, stirring occasionally, for 1-2 minutes, until the chorizo begins to crisp. Add the rice and turmeric and cook, stirring, for 2 minutes, then add the drained chopped tomatoes, pepper, garlic, chilli and stock. Bring to the boil, then reduce the heat to medium-low and cook, stirring occasionally for 15 minutes or until all the liquid has been absorbed.

Return the chicken to the pan with the prawns, cannellini beans and green beans. Toss and heat through for 1 minute.

Stir in the coriander and serve immediately with the lemon wedges as a garnish.

*Chorizo, a Spanish spicy sausage, is available from delis and selected supermarkets.

Serves 4-6

5 OF THE BEST
vegetarian mains

rosemary veggie **kebabs**
with seasoned rice

1 red onion, cut into 2cm pieces
1 green courgette, thickly sliced
1 yellow courgette, thickly sliced
8 fresh shiitake mushrooms, halved if large
1 red pepper, cut into 2cm pieces
1 yellow pepper, cut into 2cm pieces
16 cherry tomatoes
40ml extra-virgin olive oil
40ml balsamic vinegar
1 tsp vegetable stock powder
200g brown rice
30g unsalted butter
1 heaped tbsp finely chopped
    flat-leaf parsley
8 long rosemary sprigs*
tomato chutney, to serve

Place all the vegetables in a bowl along with the tomatoes, olive oil and vinegar, then toss to combine. Set aside for 10 minutes.

Fill a large saucepan with cold water and add the vegetable stock powder, then bring to the boil. Add the brown rice and simmer for 20 minutes, then drain. Return the rice to the pan, add the butter, and season with salt and pepper. Stir in the parsley, then cover and keep warm.

Strip almost all the rosemary leaves from the sprigs, leaving just the top leaves (reserve these for use in other dishes). Wrap the top leaves in foil, then thread the vegetables, alternating varieties, onto the sprigs.

Preheat a chargrill or barbecue to medium-high and cook the kebabs for 4-5 minutes, turning, until the vegetables are lightly charred and just tender. Serve with rice and tomato chutney.

*Alternatively, use wooden skewers that have been soaked in cold water for 15 minutes.

Serves 4

pea & haloumi fritters

250g frozen peas
125ml milk
2 eggs
30g cornflour
100g plain flour
½ tsp baking powder
250g haloumi cheese,
    cut into 1cm cubes
1 heaped tbsp chopped mint,
    plus extra to serve
olive oil, to shallow-fry
roasted vine-ripened truss tomatoes, mint
    leaves and lemon wedges, to serve

Boil the peas in salted water for 2 minutes, then drain. Refresh under cold water, then drain again. Purée half the peas in a food processor until smooth.

Whisk the milk, eggs, flours, baking powder and puréed peas in a bowl, then fold in the remaining peas, haloumi, mint, salt and pepper.

Heat the olive oil in a large non-stick frying pan over a medium-high heat. Add a tablespoon of the mixture to the pan, in batches, pressing down to flatten slightly, and fry for 2-3 minutes, or until golden on both sides. Drain on paper towels.

Serve with the tomatoes, mint and lemon wedges.

Serves 4

lentil & cauliflower pilaf

2 tbsp vegetable or groundnut oil
1 small onion, finely chopped
450g cauliflower (about ½), cut into florets
250g basmati rice
2 heaped tbsp mild curry paste
    (such as korma)
750ml vegetable stock
2 bay leaves
1 cinnamon stick
1 x 400g can lentils, drained, rinsed
2 heaped tbsp finely chopped
    coriander leaves
mango chutney, to serve (optional)

Heat the oil in a large frying pan over a medium heat.

Add the onion and cook for 5 minutes, stirring occasionally. Add the cauliflower and rice and cook, stirring, for 2 minutes. Add the curry paste and cook for a further minute. Add the stock, bay leaves and cinnamon, then bring to the boil.

Reduce the heat to low, cover and cook for 15 minutes, or until the rice is cooked and all the liquid has been absorbed.

Fluff the rice with a fork, stir in the lentils and heat through for 1 minute.

Sprinkle on the chopped coriander, and serve with chutney, if desired.

Serves 6

oven-roasted **veggies** with **feta** dressing

2 red peppers, seeds and
  membrane removed
2 courgettes (1 yellow, 1 green)
¼ butternut squash
40ml extra-virgin olive oil
1 bunch asparagus, trimmed
12 cherry tomatoes on the vine

for the feta dressing
150g reduced-fat feta cheese
80ml skim milk
60ml olive oil
2 garlic cloves

Preheat the oven to 190°C/375°F/gas mark 5.

Lightly grease a baking tray.

Cut the peppers, courgettes and squash into large chunks and toss with half the oil. Season with salt and pepper.

Place the squash on the tray and roast for 15 minutes. Add the peppers and courgettes and roast for 10 minutes.

Brush the asparagus and tomatoes with the remaining oil, add to the tray and cook for a further 8 minutes. Remove and allow the vegetables to cool.

To make the dressing, blend the ingredients in a food processor until smooth.

To serve, place the vegetables on a platter with the dressing in a bowl on the side.

Serves 4

baked **aubergine** with **goat cheese** & cream

2 medium aubergines
30ml olive oil
3 garlic cloves, crushed
300ml good-quality passata
250ml double cream
1 heaped tbsp each chopped
  fresh basil, mint and thyme
150g soft goat cheese

Cut the aubergines into 2.5cm slices, sprinkle with salt and place in a colander. Set aside for 30 minutes (the salt leaches out any bitterness and excess liquid). Rinse and pat dry with paper towels.

Preheat the oven to 180°C/350°F/gas mark 4.

Brush the aubergine with the oil. Heat a chargrill pan over a high heat. When hot, add the aubergine and grill for 1-2 minutes each side (it doesn't need to cook right through). Drain on paper towels.

Put the garlic and passata in a bowl and stir to combine. In a separate bowl, combine the cream and herbs and season with salt and pepper.

Place 4 slices of aubergine in the base of a small baking dish, then spread with half the cheese. Top with a little tomato mixture, then another layer of aubergine. Repeat with the remaining ingredients.

Pour the cream over the top and bake for 15 minutes. Serve immediately.

Serves 4

5 OF THE BEST
salads

the new **greek** salad

120ml extra-virgin olive oil
40ml balsamic vinegar
1 x 200g bag mixed salad leaves
250g small roma tomatoes, halved,
  seeded, chopped
2 lebanese cucumbers*, peeled,
  halved, seeded, sliced
1 small red onion, thinly sliced
80g small kalamata olives
250g marinated feta cheese, crumbled
75g fresh or frozen redcurrants
12 large sardines, cleaned, gutted
olive oil, to brush
lemon wedges, to serve
chopped flat-leaf parsley, to garnish

Whisk the oil and vinegar together, season, then set aside at room temperature.

Put the salad leaves, tomato, cucumber, onion, olives, half the feta and redcurrants in a separate bowl. Season to taste with salt and black pepper.

Brush the sardines with olive oil and grill for 2-3 minutes each side, until just cooked.

Toss the salad with the dressing, then divide among six plates. Top each plate with sardines.

Garnish with the lemon wedges, the remaining feta and chopped parsley.

*Lebanese cucumbers are small, thin-skinned cucumbers, usually no more than 15cm long. Use small cucumbers if unavailable.

Serves 6

quail salad with chinese marbled eggs

Begin this recipe the day before.

12 quail eggs*
2 tsp sea salt
125ml light soy sauce
125ml dark soy sauce
6 star anise
20g (approximately) or 8 tea bags
    lapsang souchong tea leaves*,
    or 8 tea bags
50g palm sugar*, grated
1 tsp turmeric
2.5cm fresh ginger, peeled, grated
4 garlic cloves, sliced
120ml white wine
6 quail
150g shiitake mushrooms
40ml sunflower oil
200g-240g mixed asian salad
    leaves (or micro mixed
    lettuce leaves)

for the palm sugar dressing
4 tbsp palm sugar*
1 garlic clove, crushed
1 tsp sea salt
40ml red-wine vinegar
80ml olive oil

Place the eggs in a pan of cold water. Bring to the boil. Reduce the heat to low and simmer for 12 minutes. Drain; cool slightly. Tap the eggs all around to crack the shell, but don't remove.

Place the eggs, salt, 80ml light soy and 80ml dark soy in the saucepan with 4 star anise and the tea leaves. Cover the eggs with cold water. Bring to the boil. Reduce the heat to low and simmer for 2 hours (top up with water if necessary). Cool, then put the mixture into a bowl. Refrigerate for at least 8 hours.

Put the remaining soy and star anise, the sugar, turmeric, ginger, garlic, wine and 1 litre of water in a pan. Bring to the boil, then reduce the heat to low and simmer for 1 hour. Add the quail, return to the boil then remove from the heat and allow to cool in the liquid. (The quail and eggs can be prepared to this stage the day before). When nearly ready to serve, peel the eggs, discard the shells and keep refrigerated.

To make the dressing, put the palm sugar and 60ml water in a small saucepan over a medium heat, stirring to dissolve the sugar. Increase the heat to high and cook until reduced by half, then set aside to cool. Add the remaining dressing ingredients and whisk to combine.

Preheat the oven to 200°C/400°F/gas mark 6. Bring the quail to room temperature and toss it with the shiitake in the oil. Transfer the quail to a roasting tray and cook in the oven for 5 minutes, until golden. Set aside. Roast the shiitake in the oven for 2 minutes. Place the salad in a bowl. Carve each quail into 4 joints, add to the salad and toss through the dressing. Divide among plates or pile onto a platter. Top with eggs.

*Quail eggs are available from good delis and some poultry suppliers. Lapsang souchong is a black Chinese tea with a smoky flavour and is available from major supermarkets. Palm sugar can be found in Asian supermarkets.

Serves 6-8

thai beef salad

400g piece eye fillet
2 heaped tbsp crushed
  black peppercorns
1 tsp five-spice powder
20ml vegetable oil
100g rice vermicelli
1 heaped tbsp brown sugar
60ml lime juice
60ml fish sauce
1 long red chilli, deseeded,
  cut into long strips
150g packet mixed asian greens
2 lebanese cucumbers, cut into
  strips
Thai basil leaves* and chopped
  peanuts, to garnish

Preheat oven to 200°C/400°F/gas mark 6.

Pat the beef dry with paper towels. Mix the peppercorns and five-spice powder and press on the beef. Heat the oil in a frying pan over a high heat and sear the beef all over. Place on a baking tray in the oven for 6 minutes. Set aside; the meat will be very rare.

Soak the vermicelli in boiling water for 2 minutes, then drain, refresh with cold water and drain again. Divide among four serving bowls.

In a separate bowl, combine the sugar, lime juice, fish sauce and chilli.

Wash and dry the greens, then pile them onto the noodles along with the cucumber. Thinly slice the beef and place it on the greens. Drizzle with dressing. Top with basil and peanuts.

*Thai basil is available from Asian supermarkets; substitute with common basil if not available. Lebanese cucumbers are small, thin-skinned cucumbers.

Serves 4

smoked chicken, cherry & avocado salad

80ml light soy sauce
juice of 1 lime
20ml mirin*
50ml olive oil
20ml balsamic vinegar
1 smoked chicken or 4 smoked chicken
   breasts, meat shredded
225g cherries
2 avocados, flesh chopped
100g baby rocket leaves
80g whole almonds
1 small red onion, thinly sliced

Put the soy, lime juice, mirin, oil and vinegar in a screwtop jar. Shake well and season to taste with salt and pepper.

In a large bowl, toss the chicken, cherries, avocado, rocket and almonds with the dressing.

Place on plates and top with onion.

* Mirin or rice wine is available from Asian supermarkets.

Serves 4

crumbed bocconcini & roast tomato salad

150g plain flour
140g dried breadcrumbs
   (200g packaged)
2 eggs
220g cherry (baby) bocconcini
   (*see* p. 11)
80ml extra-virgin olive oil
1 garlic clove, crushed
20ml balsamic vinegar
1 tsp dijon mustard
16 roasted roma tomato halves*
   or 75g sun-dried tomatoes in oil
125g wild rocket
2 heaped tbsp toasted pine nuts
vegetable oil, to deep-fry

Place the flour and breadcrumbs on separate sheets of baking paper. Beat the eggs together in a bowl.

Drain the bocconcini and pat dry with paper towel. Dip each ball first in the flour, then in the egg, then in the breadcrumbs, coating well. Chill for 15 minutes.

Meanwhile, shake the olive oil, garlic, vinegar, mustard, and salt and pepper in a screw-top jar. Set aside.

Put the tomatoes, rocket leaves and pine nuts in a serving bowl.

Half-fill a deep-fryer or large, heavy-based saucepan with vegetable oil and heat to 190°C/375°F/gas mark 5. (If you don't have a deep-fryer thermometer, test a cube of bread; it will turn golden in 30 seconds when the oil is hot enough.)

Fry the bocconcini, in two batches, for 1-2 minutes until crisp and golden. Drain on paper towel, then add to the serving bowl. Drizzle with dressing and serve immediately.

*Available from selected delicatessens.

Serves 4

5 OF THE BEST
potatoes

creamy **mashed** potato

8 large potatoes (such as desiree),
    peeled, cut into chunks
300ml single cream
100g butter, plus extra to serve
sea salt and black pepper

Place the potato pieces in a saucepan of cold water. Bring to the boil and cook for 10 minutes, or until tender. Remove from the heat, drain and use a potato masher or fork to mash.

Heat the cream and butter in a saucepan over a medium heat until the mixture is hot (don't allow it to boil) and the butter has melted. Use a whisk to slowly beat the cream mixture into the potatoes until smooth.

Season to taste with sea salt and black pepper. Serve with the extra butter.

Serves 4

potato pancakes with smoked salmon

450g desiree potatoes,
    peeled and diced
1 heaped tbsp plain flour
3 eggs
1 egg white
50ml double cream
50ml milk
grated fresh nutmeg,
    to season
40ml vegetable oil
sour cream, smoked salmon
    and lumpfish roe*, to serve
chopped chives, to garnish

Preheat the oven to 110°C/°225°F/gas mark ¼.

Boil or steam the potatoes until soft. Drain well. Push through a potato ricer or mash until smooth. Transfer to a large bowl, and add the flour, eggs, egg white, cream and milk. Season well with salt and pepper and grated nutmeg and stir well.

Heat the oil in a small non-stick blini pan* or small frying pan. When very hot, add a quarter of the mixture. Reduce the heat to very low and cover the pan with a baking tray. Cook for 2-3 minutes each side until golden brown. Place on a baking tray in the oven while you cook the remaining pancakes.

Place a pancake on each plate, top with salmon, sour cream and roe. Garnish with chives.

*Lumpfish roe is available from some supermarkets and delis. Blini pans are available from kitchenware stores.

Serves 4

little lancashire hotpots

2 x 500g lamb fillets,
    fat trimmed, sinew removed
40ml olive oil
1 onion, thinly sliced
1 large carrot, peeled,
    finely chopped
2 celery stalks, finely diced
6 small mushrooms, sliced
1 heaped tbsp plain flour
150ml white wine
150ml chicken or lamb stock
25g pearl barley
110g king edward potatoes,
    peeled, very thinly sliced
25g butter, melted

Preheat the oven to 170°C/°325°F/gas mark 3.

Cut the lamb into small pieces. Heat half the oil in a frying pan, add the lamb and fry in batches until sealed and light brown. Place a few pieces in each ramekin.

Heat the remaining oil in the pan, add the onion and cook over a medium heat for 1-2 minutes until just starting to brown. Add the carrot, celery and mushrooms, and cook for a further minute. Add the flour and stir in well before adding the wine and stock. Finally, add the barley, season well with salt and pepper, then divide among the ramekins.

Arrange the potatoes on top, brush with butter and place a circle of non-stick baking paper over each pot. Place in a roasting pan, cover the pan with foil and bake for 1½ hours. (If making in advance, set aside to cool after baking, then refrigerate.) Remove the foil and baking paper, brush with a bit more butter and bake, uncovered, for 30 minutes.

Serves 6

spicy potatoes with poppadams

750g potatoes, peeled, cubed
4 tbsp ghee*
1/2 tsp turmeric
2 heaped tbsp *panch phora*
1 heaped tbsp ground cumin
6 fresh curry leaves*
1 garlic clove, crushed
1 heaped tbsp grated
   fresh ginger
6 large poppadams
60ml lemon juice
20g (approximately) chopped
   fresh coriander
tomato *kasundi** and yoghurt,
   if desired, to serve

Put the potatoes in a saucepan of salted water and bring to the boil (alternatively, steam them). Cook until just tender. Drain and set aside.

Heat a tablespoon of the ghee in a medium frying pan. Add the dry spices, curry leaves, garlic and ginger and cook over a medium heat for 1 minute, stirring until the flavours are released. Transfer to a bowl and set aside.

Add 1 tablespoon of ghee to the pan; when it has melted, add the potatoes (in 2 batches if necessary) and cook until golden. Return the spice mixture to the pan and cook for a further minute. Cover and set aside.

Heat the remaining ghee in a small frying pan over high heat. Carefully place 1 poppadam in the hot oil (press with tongs to help hold the shape) and fry for 2-3 seconds each side, until fully expanded. Use tongs to transfer it to paper towels to drain. Repeat with remaining poppadams.

Add the lemon juice and coriander to the potatoes and reheat gently over a low heat for 1-2 minutes.

Place a poppadam on a serving plate, top with some spicy potatoes and the tomato *kasundi*. Add a dollop of yoghurt.

* Ghee is clarified butter, available from supermarkets. *Panch phora* is an Indian spice mix available from spice stores. Curry leaves are available from good greengrocers. Tomato *kasundi* is a spicy Indian chutney available at Asian supermarkets.

Serves 6

tartiflette

This cheese-and-potato bake recipe originates in France.

1kg potatoes, peeled,
  roughly chopped
50g unsalted butter
1 onion, chopped
2 garlic cloves, finely chopped
2 tsp chopped thyme
200g *speck** or pancetta,
  cut into 1cm dice
125ml dry white wine
200ml double cream
250g raclette* or reblochon*
  cheese, grated

Preheat the oven to 200°C/400°F/gas mark 6.

Place the potato in a large saucepan, cover with cold salted water and bring to a boil over a high heat. Boil for 3 minutes, then drain well.

Melt the butter in a large frying pan over a medium-low heat. Add the onion and cook, stirring occasionally, for 5 minutes, or until onion is soft. Add the garlic, thyme and *Speck* or pancetta, and cook, stirring, for 5 minutes. Add the white wine, cream, most of the cheese and the potato, and stir to combine.

Transfer the potato mixture to a large baking dish and sprinkle over the remaining cheese. Cover with a sheet of non-stick baking paper to prevent the cheese sticking, then add a layer of foil. Bake for 20 minutes, then remove the foil and baking paper. Bake for a further 20 minutes, or until bubbling and golden. Serve tartiflette with venison.

*Speck, a German-style smoked bacon, is available from selected supermarkets, delicatessens and butchers; substitute streaky bacon if you can't find it. Raclette and reblochon cheese are available from delicatessens and specialty cheese shops; substitute Gruyère.

Serves 4-6

5 OF THE BEST
vegetables

parmesan carrots with aioli

500g baby carrots, peeled
250g fresh white breadcrumbs
2 tsp grated lemon zest
¼ tsp dried chilli flakes
2 heaped tbsp finely chopped
   flat-leaf parsley
2 heaped tbsp finely
   grated parmesan
75g plain flour
2 eggs, beaten
500ml vegetable or peanut oil, to fry
aioli, to serve

for the aioli
2 garlic cloves
3 egg yolks
½ tsp dijon mustard
60ml vegetable or groundnut oil
125ml extra-virgin olive oil
juices of 1 lemon

Remove the carrot tops, leaving a little stalk.

Bring a large saucepan of salted water to the boil, add the carrots and cook for 3 minutes. Drain and then dry on paper towels.

Combine the breadcrumbs, zest, chilli, parsley and Parmesan, and season. Put the flour and eggs in separate bowls. Roll the carrots first in flour, then in the egg and then cover in breadcrumbs.

Fry the carrots in hot oil for 1-2 minutes until crisp. Drain on paper towel. Serve with aioli.

Serves 4

Aioli
Place the garlic in a food processor along with the egg yolks and Dijon mustard, and process to combine. While processing, slowly add the oils, lemon juice, and salt and pepper to taste until combined.

fennel with orange & olives

4 heads baby fennel
30ml olive oil
2 cloves garlic, finely chopped
2 oranges
250ml chicken or
    vegetable stock
120g pitted black olives

Remove the fronds from the fennel. Finely chop the fronds and set aside. Cut each fennel bulb into quarters.

Juice one orange and cut the other into quarters, then slice each quarter.

Heat the oil in a deep frying pan, add the fennel and cook, turning from time to time until the vegetables are golden and starting to soften. Add the garlic, stirring to combine.

Add the orange juice and stock and bring to the boil, then turn the heat to low and simmer covered for 5-6 minutes.

Remove the lid and add the orange slices and olives, cook for a further 1-2 minutes. Stir in the reserved fennel fronds.

Serve as part of an antipasto or with grilled fish.

Serves 4

broad beans with pangrattato

Pangrattato is breadcrumbs fried in garlic oil. In Italy, it was used as a traditional substitute and cheap alternative for Parmesan because it has a similar texture.

500g fresh or frozen broad beans
40ml olive oil
35g fresh breadcrumbs
2 tsp grated lemon rind
1 garlic clove, crushed
2 heaped tbsp grated parmesan

Cook the beans in boiling salted water until just tender. Drain, then refresh under cold water. Remove the outer shell from the beans. Discard the outer shells.

To make the *pangrattato*, heat 20ml of the olive oil in a frying pan over a medium heat, add the breadcrumbs and cook, stirring occasionally, until the breadcrumbs are golden. Add the lemon rind and garlic and stir to combine. Remove from the heat and set aside. Wipe the pan clean.

Place the remaining oil in the pan over a medium heat, add the beans and toss until warmed through. Season with salt and pepper. Place in a serving bowl and sprinkle with the Parmesan and the *pangrattato*.

Note: The beans can be boiled and peeled several hours before cooking.

Serves 4-6 as a side dish

chickpeas with spinach

1 x 425g can chickpeas
450g baby spinach
40ml olive oil
3 garlic cloves, crushed
1-2 slices white bread, cubed,
    crusts removed
1 tsp mild paprika
1/2 tsp ground cumin
250ml chicken stock

Rinse and drain the chickpeas, then set aside.

Wash the baby spinach, then steam until just wilted. Squeeze out the excess water, then roughly chop and set aside.

Heat the olive oil in a skillet over a medium heat, add the garlic cloves and cook for 1 minute. Add the white bread cubes, the paprika and ground cumin and cook until the bread is crisp.

Place the bread mixture in a blender, add the chicken stock and blend to a paste.

Transfer the spinach to a bowl along with the paste and chickpeas and toss to combine.

Serve at room temperature.

Serves 4-6

peperonata

60ml olive oil
2 large onions, thinly sliced
2 garlic cloves, crushed
2 red peppers, seeds removed, cut into thin strips
2 yellow peppers, seeds removed, cut into thin strips
6 large vine-ripened tomatoes, peeled, deseeded, sliced
4 anchovy fillets, drained, finely chopped
pinch of sugar

Heat the oil in a large saucepan, add the onions and cook over a low heat until very soft and starting to caramelize. Add the garlic and peppers and cook another 10-15 minutes, stirring from time to time.

Add the tomatoes and anchovies, and sweeten with a pinch of sugar, then season with salt and pepper. Simmer for 35-40 minutes, stirring occasionally, until thick.

Serve at room temperature.

Serves 8

5 OF THE BEST
white fish

pan-fried fish with black-bean dressing

8 x 150g skinless white fish fillets
    (such as bream or john dory)
2 heaped tbsp plain flour,
    seasoned with salt and pepper
40ml olive or groundnut oil
steamed jasmine rice, to serve

for the black bean dressing
50g brown sugar
2 tsp each fish sauce and
    sesame oil
20ml light soy sauce
80ml olive oil
zest and juice of 3 limes
4 tbsp salted black
    beans*, rinsed
1 long red chilli, seeds
    removed, sliced
1 red onion, thinly sliced
2 heaped tbsp chopped coriander,
    plus extra leaves to serve

Combine all the dressing ingredients. Set aside.

Lightly dust the fish in the flour.

Heat the oil in a non-stick pan over a medium-low heat
and cook the fish for 2 minutes each side, or until light golden
and cooked through.

Serve the fish on a bed of steamed rice, pour on the dressing
and garnish with the extra coriander.

* Available from Asian food shops.

Serves 4

fish with asparagus & herb vinaigrette

4 (150g each) firm white fish fillets
  (such as john dory or haddock)
40ml olive oil, plus extra to brush
4 tbsp finely chopped herbs (such
  as chervil, chives and parsley)
1 heaped tbsp baby capers,
  finely chopped
a pinch of caster sugar
juice and grated rind of 1/2 lemon
1 bunch asparagus, woody ends
  trimmed, halved on the diagonal
300g marinated artichokes, drained

Preheat the oven to 180°C/350°F/gas mark 4.

Place a large frying pan over a high heat, brush the fish with a little olive oil and cook for 1-2 minutes on each side. Transfer to a baking tray and bake for 5 minutes, or until just cooked through.

Meanwhile, whisk together the olive oil, herbs, capers, sugar, lemon juice and rind in a small bowl, and season with salt and pepper.

Blanch the asparagus in a pan of boiling water for 2 minutes, then drain.

To serve, divide the asparagus and artichokes among four plates, top with the fish and drizzle with the vinaigrette.

Serves 4

fish with herb walnut crust

70g fresh white breadcrumbs
50g flat-leaf parsley leaves
2 shallots, chopped
1 clove garlic, chopped
35g walnuts, toasted
60ml walnut oil*
6 (about 150g each) sweet white
    fish fillets (such as john dory,
    haddock, sea bass, etc.)

Preheat the grill to medium and the oven to 180°C/350°F/ gas mark 4.

Lightly grease a large baking tray.

Place the breadcrumbs in a food processor together with the parsley, shallots and garlic. Process to combine, then add the toasted walnuts and pulse briefly.

Add the walnut oil and process until just combined; the texture should still be rough and the crumbs moist.

Place the fish fillets on the baking tray and spread the breadcrumb mixture on top of each piece, pressing down well to make sure the crumbs adhere.

Place the tray under the preheated grill and cook the fish for 2 minutes, until the crust just starts to turn golden. Transfer the tray to the oven and bake for 6 minutes.

Serve with pan-fried celeriac and salad.

*Walnut oil is available from delicatessens as well as selected supermarkets. Use extra-virgin olive oil if unavailable.

Serves 6

fish provençal

4 x 180g skinless white fish fillets
  (such as john dory, haddock, etc.)
20ml olive oil
1 large red onion, finely sliced
1 garlic clove, crushed
1 heaped tbsp tomato paste
1 x 425g tin chopped tomatoes
125ml white wine
1 roasted red pepper*
  (about 75g), cut into strips
12 pitted kalamata olives, halved
1 heaped tbsp chopped
  flat-leaf parsley
steamed new potatoes, to serve

Preheat the oven to 200°C/400°F/gas mark 6.

Place the fish in a lightly greased baking dish. Season, cover with foil and bake for 10-15 minutes until just cooked through.

Meanwhile, to make the sauce, heat the oil in a frying pan over a medium heat. Add the onion and stir for 1-2 minutes until it starts to soften. Add garlic and stir for a few seconds. Add the tomato paste, tomatoes and wine, then cook for 5 minutes until thickened. Add the peppers and olives, then season.

Place the fish on serving plates and pour the sauce over them. Top with parsley and serve with steamed potatoes.

*Available ready-roasted from some supermarkets and delis.

Serves 4

swordfish with agrodolce

Agrodolce is a traditional Italian sweet-and-sour sauce.

50ml olive oil
2 onions, halved, sliced
1 tsp salt
1 heaped tbsp caster sugar
1 tsp chopped fresh rosemary
80g sultanas
1 x 425g tin chopped tomatoes
grated rind and juice of 1 lemon
2 heaped tbsp chopped
   flat-leaf parsley
4 swordfish steaks
wild rocket, to serve

To make the *agrodolce*, heat 30ml of the oil in a deep frying pan. Add the onion and salt, and cook over medium heat for 1-2 minutes, stirring occasionally, until the onions start to soften but don't brown.

Add 125ml water and the sugar, cover and cook for 15 minutes until the onions are very soft. Remove the lid and cook until the onions start to brown and caramelize, then add the rosemary, sultanas, tomatoes, lemon zest and juice, and continue to cook for 3-4 minutes until quite thick. Season to taste, stir in the parsley and set aside.

Heat a chargrill or frying pan over a high heat. Season the fish with 20ml of olive oil, and some salt and pepper and cook for 2-3 minutes each side, until just cooked through. Serve with the *agrodolce*.

Serves 4

5 OF THE BEST
salmon

salmon roulade with crab sauce

6 (about 120g each) skinless salmon
  fillets, pin-boned
4 tbsp plain flour, plus 2 tsp
  extra for sauce
1 heaped tbsp sweet paprika
1 heaped tbsp dried thyme
1 tbsp ground black pepper
1 tsp salt
40ml extra-virgin olive oil
320g grape or cherry
  tomatoes, halved
1/2 tsp cayenne pepper
150ml dry white wine
250ml double cream
250g fresh crab meat
2 heaped tbsp basil leaves,
  finely sliced, plus extra leaves
  to garnish

To make the roulades, cut each fillet through the centre horizontally, nearly cutting through to the end, but stopping short so you have one long strip of fish. Starting at one end, roll each fillet into a neat round, then secure with a toothpick. Wrap each one tightly in plastic wrap and chill for at least 1 hour to firm up.

Preheat the oven to 160°C/325°F/gas mark 3.

Combine the flour, paprika, thyme, ground black pepper and salt in a bowl. Dip both flat sides of the roulades in the mixture. Heat half the oil in a non-stick frying pan over a high heat and when hot, sear the salmon on one flat side for about 1 minute or until a crust forms. Turn and repeat on the other flat side, then place on a tray in the oven for 5 minutes until just cooked.

Meanwhile, wipe the frying pan clean, heat the remaining oil and add the tomatoes. Cook over a medium-low heat, stirring, for 2-3 minutes until the tomatoes start to soften, then stir the 2 teaspoons of extra flour and the cayenne into tomato juices. Add the wine, cook for 1 minute, then add the cream and cook, stirring, for 5 minutes or until thickened. Stir in the crab to warm through, add the sliced basil, then season.

Place a little of the sauce on each plate, top with a salmon roulade and drizzle with extra crab sauce. Garnish with fresh basil leaves (and mustard cress, if desired). Serve with boiled new potatoes tossed in butter and a green salad.

Serves 6

glazed **salmon** with lime beurre blanc & tomato, **ginger** & **basil** salsa

1 (about 2-2.5kg) whole salmon or ocean trout, gutted and cleaned
vegetable or olive oil, to brush
1 lime, quartered
4 kaffir lime leaves
1 small stick lemon grass, bruised
125ml yellow sweet chilli sauce*

for the lime beurre blanc
40ml lime juice
40ml white wine
300g unsalted butter, cubed
75g salmon roe

for the tomato, ginger & basil salsa
1 heaped tbsp freshly grated ginger
40ml fish sauce
20ml seasoned rice vinegar*
1 tsp caster sugar
6 vine-ripened tomatoes, peeled, seeds removed, diced
3 spring onions, chopped
2 heaped tbsp chopped fresh basil

Preheat the oven to 180°C/350°F/gas mark 4.

Measure a piece of foil to double the length of the fish. Brush the foil with oil, then place the fish at one end. Fill the fish cavity with the lime, lime leaves and lemon grass. Brush the exposed skin of the salmon with oil. Fold the foil over, then press to seal, but allow an air pocket around the fish. Place on a large baking tray and roast for 10 minutes per 450g. Remove from the oven, then open up the foil slightly and allow to cool.

Meanwhile, to make beurre blanc, pour the lime juice and wine into a small saucepan over a medium heat. Simmer for 1 minute, then start whisking in the butter, a few pieces at a time. Continue until all the butter has been added, then season with salt and pepper. Set aside and keep warm.

To make the salsa, place the ginger, fish sauce, vinegar and sugar in a bowl and stir to dissolve the sugar. Put the tomato and shallots in a separate bowl and stir through the basil and dressing.

Cut through the skin along the back of the fish and around the head and tail. Peel away the skin and invert the fish onto a platter. Put the chilli sauce in a pan with about 80ml cold water over a low heat and simmer for 1-2 minutes, stirring to combine; brush this over the flesh of the salmon. Just before serving, stir the salmon roe into the warm beurre blanc. Serve the fish with the beurre blanc and salsa and lime wedges, if desired.

*If yellow sweet chilli sauce is unavailable, use red. Seasoned rice vinegar is available from Asian supermarkets.

Serves 6-8

salmon **rillettes** with bagel toasts

450g skinless salmon fillet,
  pin-boned
1 tbsp sea salt
125g unsalted butter, softened
6 shallots, very finely chopped
20ml crème fraîche
250g smoked trout fillet
40ml lemon juice
20ml extra-virgin olive oil
2 egg yolks
40ml pernod* (optional)
1 heaped tbsp chopped dill,
  plus a sprig to garnish
clarified butter, to top
  (*see* note)

for the bagel toasts
2 large bagels or 4 mini bagels
olive oil, to brush
1 garlic clove, halved

Place the salmon fillet in a shallow dish and sprinkle with the sea salt. Cover and refrigerate for 1 hour, turning the salmon fillet once.

Line a steamer with baking paper, then steam the salmon fillet over a saucepan of simmering water for 8 minutes until just cooked but still a little opaque in the centre. Remove the salmon and allow to cool.

Melt 40g of the butter in a frying pan over medium heat. Add the shallots and cook, stirring, for 2 minutes or until soft. Add a pinch of salt, then cook for a further 2 minutes.

Put the remaining 85g of butter in a bowl and use hand beaters to beat until pale. Add the crème fraîche and beat in well. Break the steamed salmon and smoked trout into pieces and add to the bowl with the shallots, lemon juice, oil, and egg yolks, Pernod (if using) and dill. Beat gently until the mixture is combined but still coarse, then season well. Place in a glass bowl or clip-lock jar large enough to fit all the mixture and cover with a 1cm layer of cooled clarified butter (*see* Note, below). Top with the dill sprig, then cover with plastic wrap or the jar lid and chill for at least 1 hour. (The rillettes will keep for three days in the fridge.)

For the bagel toasts, preheat the oven to 180°C/350°F/gas mark 4. Cut the bagels or mini-bagels into two half-rings, then slice thinly. Spread in a single layer on a baking tray, brush with olive oil and rub with the cut side of the garlic clove. Bake the bagel slices for 2-3 minutes until golden, then leave to cool. (The bagel toasts will keep in an airtight container for three days.)

Note To make the clarified butter, very gently melt 125g unsalted butter over a low heat, skimming any foam off the top but not stirring. When the butter is melted, remove from the heat and leave to stand for 1 minute, so that the milk solids settle to the bottom. Carefully pour off the golden clarified butter into a jug and discard the solids in the pan. Allow to cool before using.

*Pernod is an aniseed liqueur available from wine and spirit shops.

Serves 6-8

cajun salmon with corn salsa

1 heaped tbsp each dried thyme
  and oregano
1 tsp ground cumin
1 heaped tbsp ground coriander
1 heaped tbsp ground dried garlic
2 heaped tbsp *pimentón* (smoked paprika)
1 tbsp ground white pepper
2 tbsp salt
6 x 120g skinless salmon fillets
40ml olive oil
guacamole and lime wedges, to serve

for the corn salsa
40ml olive oil
cooked kernels from 2 fresh corn cobs
1 red peppers, roasted, peeled, diced
1 small red chilli, seeded, finely chopped
3 spring onions, thinly sliced
30ml lime juice
10g chopped coriander leaves

First make the salsa. Heat 2 teaspoons of oil in a non-stick pan over a high heat. When hot, fry the corn until just golden. Mix with the remaining oil and ingredients, then season.

Preheat oven to 180°C/350°F/gas mark 4.

Mix the herbs and spices with the ground white pepper and salt. Brush the salmon with 20ml of oil and coat in the spice mixture.

Heat the remaining oil in an ovenproof frying pan over a medium heat. Cook the fish for 2 minutes, then turn and cook for 1 minute. Transfer to the oven for 3-5 minutes, or until cooked.

Serve with the salsa, guacamole and lime.

Serves 6

salmon with parsnip purée

500ml orange juice
6 medium (800g) parsnips
90g butter
1 heaped tbsp grated
  orange rind
80ml single cream
2 tsp sumac*
1 tbsp plain flour
6 (about 125g each)
  salmon fillets
20ml light olive oil
125ml white wine
3 oranges, segmented
2 heaped tbsp chopped
  fresh chives

Preheat oven to 160°C/325°F/gas mark 3. Heat the orange juice over a high heat; boil for 5-6 minutes, until reduced to 100ml. Set aside.

Cook the parsnips in a large saucepan of boiling salted water until soft; drain and cool slightly. Transfer to a food processor and add salt, pepper, 75g of the butter, the orange rind and cream, and whiz until it forms a smooth purée. Set aside in a warm place.

Combine the sumac and flour on a piece of non-stick baking paper and season generously with salt and pepper. Dip the skinless side of the salmon fillets in the spice mixture to coat. Heat the remaining butter and oil in a non-stick frying pan over a medium-high heat. Add the salmon, seasoned-side down, and cook for 1 minute. Turn and cook for another minute. Transfer to a baking tray and place in the oven for 5-6 minutes. Add the wine to the orange juice and cook over a high heat for about 5 minutes until reduced by half. Add the orange segments and heat through. Stir in the chives. Put a generous serving of parsnip purée on each plate, top with a piece of salmon and drizzle with the sauce.

*Sumac is a purple, lemony spice available from Middle Eastern food stores.

Serves 6

5 OF THE BEST
chicken

chicken with pesto & mascarpone

40ml olive oil
1 onion, finely chopped
100g mild pancetta, chopped
50g grated parmesan
50g fresh white breadcrumbs
4 tbsp roughly chopped
   flat-leaf parsley leaves
1 egg
6 chicken breasts with skin
   (wing bone attached – optional)
125ml white wine
200g mascarpone
2 heaped tbsp pesto

Pour half the oil in a frying pan over a medium heat, add the onion and cook, stirring, for 2-3 minutes until soft. Add the pancetta and cook for 1-2 minutes until starting to crisp, then cool slightly. Place the mixture in a food processor with the Parmesan, breadcrumbs, parsley and egg. Pulse for just a few seconds until combined but still coarse. Season the stuffing with salt and pepper, then cool completely.

Use your fingers to gently loosen the skin of the chicken (taking care not to tear it), then carefully push the bread mixture underneath the skin. Pull the skin back over the stuffing, then place in a dish, cover and refrigerate for 30 minutes, or until the stuffing is firm.

Preheat the oven to 180°C/350°F/gas mark 4.

Heat the remaining oil in a non-stick frying pan over a medium heat. Cook the chicken skin-side down (in batches if necessary) for 1-2 minutes until golden, then turn and cook for a further 1-2 minutes. Transfer the chicken, skin-side up, to a baking tray and cook in the oven for 10 minutes, or until cooked through.

Remove and allow to rest for 5 minutes.

Meanwhile, return the pan to a medium heat, add the wine and cook until reduced by half. Turn the heat to low, stir in the mascarpone and heat through, then stir in the pesto.

Place the chicken breasts on plates and drizzle over some sauce – serve any remaining sauce on the side. Serve with potatoes, beans and peas.

Serves 6

chicken **cacciatore**

60ml olive oil
6 chicken drumsticks, excess fat removed, skin on
6 chicken thighs, excess fat removed, skin on
1 large onion, chopped
2 celery sticks, chopped
2 carrots, peeled and chopped
150g sliced pancetta, chopped
3 garlic cloves, crushed
125g button mushrooms, sliced
100ml dry white wine
1 x 800g can chopped tomatoes
1/2 tsp brown sugar
20ml balsamic vinegar
1 heaped tbsp chopped fresh rosemary
1 bay leaf
150ml chicken stock
150g pitted kalamata olives
chopped flat-leaf parsley, to garnish

Heat the olive oil in a large casserole dish over a medium-high heat.

Add the chicken pieces and cook until browned all over. Transfer to a plate and set aside.

Add the onion, celery, carrot and pancetta to the pan and cook over low heat for 5 minutes, or until the onion softens. Add the garlic and mushrooms and cook for a further minute.

Return the chicken pieces to the pan, add the wine and allow to simmer 1-2 minutes. Add the tomatoes, sugar, vinegar, herbs and stock.

Bring to the boil, then reduce the heat to low and cook, covered, for 20 minutes, stirring occasionally. Add the olives and cook for a further 10 minutes.

Transfer the chicken to a platter, then reduce the sauce over a high heat for 5-6 minutes. Serve garnished with the parsley.

Serves 6

simple **moroccan** chicken

500g chicken fillet, cut into 2cm dice
4 tbsp flour, seasoned with
   salt and pepper
60ml olive oil
2 onions, sliced
2 tsp ground cinnamon
1/4 tsp ground cloves
2 tsp sumac*
4 tbsp sultanas
250ml chicken stock
50g toasted pine nuts*
4 tbsp chopped fresh coriander
juice of 1 lemon, plus wedges to serve
couscous, greek yoghurt and
   lebanese bread, to serve

Toss the chicken in the seasoned flour. Heat 40ml of the olive oil in a large frying pan over a high heat until hot, then cook the chicken in batches until golden and set aside.

Heat the remaining oil in the pan. Add the onions, reduce the heat to medium and cook for 10 minutes, stirring, until golden and softened.

Return the chicken to the pan and add the spices, sultanas and stock. Reduce the heat to low and cook for 5 minutes until heated through and thickened slightly. Stir in the pine nuts, coriander and lemon juice.

Serve with couscous, yoghurt, bread and lemon.

*Sumac is a purple, lemony spice used in North African and Middle Eastern cooking. It is available from ethnic food shops and selected delis. Ready-toasted pine nuts are available from supermarkets.

Serves 4

minced chicken with thai basil

20ml vegetable oil
4 garlic cloves, chopped
1 tsp grated ginger
1 long red chilli, seeds removed, chopped, plus extra finely sliced chilli, to serve
500g chicken breast mince
4 kaffir lime leaves*, finely sliced
40ml fish sauce
20ml oyster sauce
20ml *kecap manis**
1 heaped tbsp brown sugar
200ml chicken stock
60g thai basil leaves*
2 heaped tbsp chopped roasted peanuts
4 spring onions, thinly sliced
leaves from 1 butter (or round) lettuce
boiled jasmine rice, to serve (optional)

Heat the oil in a wok over a medium-high heat. Add the garlic, ginger and chilli and cook for 1 minute.

Increase the heat to high, add the chicken and cook, stirring constantly, for 5-6 minutes, until it is cooked through. Add the shredded lime leaves, fish and oyster sauces, *kecap manis*, brown sugar and stock, and cook for a further 1-2 minutes.

Remove from the heat and stir in the basil and nuts. Serve the chicken on lettuce leaves topped with spring onion and chilli, accompanied by boiled rice, if desired.

*Kaffir lime leaves and Thai basil are available from selected greengrocers and Asian food shops; substitute common basil for Thai basil if unavailable. *Kecap manis* is Indonesian sweet soy sauce, available from Asian food shops.

Serves 4

chicken with peaches & vanilla

4 chicken breasts, preferably
    corn-fed, with skin (wing-bone
    attached, optional)
20ml olive oil
4 tbsp light muscovado
    or brown sugar
4 small peaches, skinned
600ml muscat or sweet white wine
125ml chicken stock
2 vanilla pods, split, seeds
    scraped and reserved
watercress, to garnish

Preheat the oven to 200°C/400°F/gas mark 6.

Season the chicken. Heat the oil in an ovenproof frying pan over a medium heat. Cook the chicken skin-side down for 2-3 minutes, until golden. Cook for 1 minute on the other side. Place the pan in the oven for 8 minutes.

Sprinkle the chicken with sugar and add the peaches, wine, stock and vanilla pods and seeds to the pan. Return the pan to the oven for 8 minutes, or until the chicken is cooked through, basting twice with the pan juices. Remove the chicken and peaches from the pan and keep warm. Return the pan to the stove and simmer the cooking juices over a medium heat for 2-3 minutes to reduce.

Serve the chicken with the peaches and vanilla sauce. Garnish with watercress.

Serves 4

5 OF THE BEST
pork

spanish pork

1 heaped tbsp mustard
1 garlic clove, crushed
1 heaped tbsp baby capers,
   rinsed and drained
8 pimento-stuffed green
   olives, sliced
1 heaped tbsp chopped
   flat-leaf parsley
grated zest and juice of 1 lemon
30ml olive oil
350g piece pork fillet, trimmed
cooked broad beans, to serve

Preheat the oven to 180°C/350°F/gas mark 4.

To make the sauce, whisk together the mustard, garlic, capers, olives, parsley, lemon zest and juice, 20ml of the olive oil, pepper to taste and 40ml of warm water.

Heat the remaining oil in an ovenproof frying pan over a high heat and cook the pork, turning, for 5 minutes until golden. Place the pan in the oven for 5 minutes until pork is cooked through.

Rest pork for 5 minutes, then slice.

Drizzle with the sauce and serve with broad beans.

Serves 2

tuscan pork
with warm fig salsa

2 garlic cloves, crushed
60ml olive oil
1 tbsp sea salt
1 heaped tbsp dried oregano
2 heaped tbsp finely
    chopped rosemary
1 heaped tbsp fennel seeds, crushed
1 tsp dried chilli flakes
2-2.5kg pork loin, boned and tied*
1 heaped tbsp plain flour
200ml chicken stock
200g baby dried figs*, quartered
120ml dry marsala
1 heaped tbsp finely chopped
    flat-leaf parsley

Preheat the oven to 200°C/400°F/gas mark 6.

Place the garlic, oil, salt, some pepper, oregano, rosemary, fennel seeds and chilli in a bowl and stir to combine. Place the pork loin in a roasting pan and rub all over with the herb mix.

Place the pork in the oven and cook for 30 minutes, reduce the heat to 170°C/325°F/gas mark 3 and roast for a further 2-2½ hours. The skin should be crisp and the juices should run clear. Remove the pork and set aside to rest.

Drain the pan of excess fat, place the roasting pan over a low heat, add the flour and cook, stirring, for 2-3 minutes, until the flour becomes golden brown. Add the chicken stock and cook, stirring, until the sauce thickens. Strain the sauce and wipe the pan clean with paper towels.

Return the sauce to the pan, add the figs and marsala and reduce until quite thick and syrupy. Season with salt and pepper and add the parsley.

Carve the pork into thick slices and serve with a little of the fig salsa.

*Ask your butcher to prepare the pork loin. Baby dried figs are available from good delicatessens and Middle-Eastern stores.

Serves 6

pork fillet with cherry sauce

2 x 300g pork fillets
20ml olive oil, plus extra
    for brushing
1 heaped tbsp
    chopped rosemary
24 thin slices flat pancetta*
    or streaky bacon
150ml dry red wine
150ml cranberry juice
6½ tbsp cherry jam
    (preferably morello*)
1 tsp balsamic vinegar
1 tsp cornflour
fresh cherries, to garnish
    (when in season)

Preheat the oven to 180°C/350°F/gas mark 4.

Cut the pork fillets in half to make four pieces. Brush with a little olive oil, season to taste with salt and pepper, then roll each fillet in the chopped rosemary leaves.

Lay out 6 slices of pancetta or bacon, slightly overlapping, on a board. Place a piece of pork on top and wrap in the pancetta, pressing to enclose. Repeat with the remaining pancetta and pork.

For the cherry sauce, put the wine, cranberry juice, cherry jam and 150ml water in a small saucepan. Simmer over a medium heat, stirring, for 5 minutes. Add the vinegar and simmer for a further minute. Mix the cornflour with a little water to form a paste. Add to the sauce and cook for about 1 minute or until thickened. Set aside.

Heat a large frying pan over a high heat. Add the oil and cook the pork fillets, turning occasionally, for 3-4 minutes until golden all over. Place on a baking tray and transfer to the oven for 5 minutes, or until the pork is cooked through.

Gently reheat the sauce while you leave the pork to rest for 2-3 minutes.

Slice the pork and serve with the cherry sauce, accompanied by mashed potato and a rocket salad. Garnish with fresh cherries if available.

*Flat pancetta is from selected delis. Morello cherry jam is available from gourmet food shops and delis.

Serves 4

rack of pork with cider apples

2kg rack of pork
olive oil, to rub
sea salt
1kg granny smith apples,
   peeled, cored, cut into
   thick wedges
80g caster sugar
1 cinnamon stick
2 tsp chopped sage
400ml good-quality
   apple cider
100g unsalted
   butter, chopped
200ml good-quality
   chicken stock
roasted parsnips
   and steamed broccoli,
   to serve

Preheat the oven to 220°C/425°F/gas mark 7. Place the pork in a roasting pan, skin-side up, then rub the skin with a little oil and sprinkle generously with sea salt. Roast for 15 minutes, then reduce oven temperature to 180°C/350°F/gas mark 4 and roast for 1¼-1½ hours, or until the juices run clear from the thickest part.

Meanwhile, cook the apples, sugar, cinnamon, sage and 200ml of the cider in a saucepan over a low heat, covered, for 20-25 minutes until the apple is soft. Allow to cool slightly. Discard the cinnamon stick, then process the mixture in a food processor with 50g of the butter until smooth (you may need to add more sugar, depending on the tartness of the apples).

When the pork is cooked, transfer it to a platter, cover loosely with foil and set aside. Skim any excess fat from the pan juices and place the pan over a medium heat. Add the stock and remaining cider and cook for 2-3 minutes, stirring and scraping any brown bits from the base of the pan. Whisk in the remaining 50g butter, then strain into a jug.

Carve the pork and serve with the puréed cider apples, gravy, roasted parsnips and steamed broccoli.

Serves 6

pork with **strawberry balsamic** sauce

250g strawberries
60ml good-quality
  balsamic vinegar
2 tsp caster sugar
4 (about 220g each) pork cutlets
40ml olive oil
60ml chicken stock
dressed mixed salad leaves,
  to serve
20g shredded basil leaves,
  to garnish

Preheat the oven to 200°C/400°F/gas mark 6.

Halve the strawberries and place in a glass or ceramic bowl with the vinegar and sugar, then set aside for 15 minutes.

Season the pork cutlets with salt and pepper. Heat the oil in an ovenproof frying pan over a medium-high heat. When hot, sear the cutlets until golden on both sides. Transfer to the oven and cook for 10 minutes. Transfer to a plate and cover loosely with foil, then allow to rest for 5 minutes.

Place the frying pan over a medium heat and add the stock. Deglaze the pan, then bring to the boil. Add the strawberry mixture, reduce the heat to low and just heat through. Season with salt and pepper.

Divide the pork cutlets and salad leaves among serving plates. Top the pork with the sauce and sprinkle with the basil.

Serves 4

5 OF THE BEST
lamb

lamb **shanks** french **daube-style**

60ml olive oil
120g mild pancetta, chopped
2 large onions, finely sliced
6 garlic cloves, crushed
4 carrots, peeled, sliced
12 frenched* lamb shanks
seasoned flour
1 x 75cl bottle red wine
600ml tomato passata
200ml beef stock
1 bouquet garni*

for the mustard mash
1kg desiree potatoes, peeled
200ml milk, warmed
50g unsalted butter
2 heaped tbsp
   wholegrain mustard
1 heaped tbsp dijon mustard

Preheat oven to 170°C/325°F/gas mark 3.

Heat 20ml of the oil in a large ovenproof casserole dish over a medium heat. Add the pancetta and cook for 2-3 minutes. Add the onion, garlic and carrot and cook for about 5 minutes, stirring occasionally. Once the mixture starts to colour, remove and set aside.

Toss the lamb in the seasoned flour. Heat the remaining oil in the casserole dish, add the lamb and fry for 2-3 minutes, until light golden all over. Set aside.

Return the vegetables to the pan, add the wine and bring to the boil for 2-3 minutes, then add the passata and stock. Season, then add the bouquet garni. Bring back to the boil, then remove from the heat, cover and place in the oven for 2½ hours. Remove and set aside for 10 minutes.

Meanwhile, make the mustard mash. Put the potatoes in a pan of cold salted water, bring to the boil, then simmer for 10 minutes until just tender. Drain and mash, then, using a wooden spoon, slowly beat in the warm milk and butter until smooth and creamy. Season with salt and pepper and stir in both mustards.

Use paper towels to dab off any excess fat that may have risen to the surface of the lamb shanks. Serve with the mustard mash.

Note: The shanks can be cooked the day before and refrigerated overnight. Spoon off any fat on the top, heat in a 180°C/350°F/gas mark 4 oven, stirring occasionally, for 30 minutes, until hot.

*'Frenched' is a term for cutting the meat away from the end of a bone to expose it. To make a bouquet garni, tie 1 thyme sprig, 1 bay leaf and 2-3 sprigs flat-leaf parsley together with kitchen string.

Serves 6

lamb stir-fry with coconut rice

40ml *tamari**
¼ tsp bicarbonate of soda
2 tsp cornflour
40ml sunflower oil
350g lamb loin, thinly sliced
3cm piece ginger, cut into thin strips
1 long red chilli, seeds removed,
   thinly sliced
1 carrot, peeled, cut into matchsticks
175g mange-tout, ends trimmed,
   halved diagonally
thinly sliced spring onions, to garnish

for the coconut rice
200ml coconut cream
225g basmati rice

First, make the rice by mixing the coconut cream with 180ml water. Put the rice and liquid in a large pan with 1 teaspoon salt and bring to a boil. Reduce heat to low, simmer for 10 minutes, then drain.

Meanwhile, combine the *tamari*, bicarbonate of soda and cornflour in a small bowl until smooth, then set aside.

Heat half the oil in a wok over a high heat. Cook the lamb in batches until browned; remove and set aside.

Heat the remaining oil and add the ginger, chilli and carrot. Stir-fry for 1 minute, return the lamb to the wok, add the mange-tout and tamari mixture and toss for a further minute. Serve with coconut rice and garnish with spring onions.

Tamari is wheat-free soy sauce available from selected supermarkets and health-food shops.

Serves 4

rack of lamb with chilli-mint sauce

40ml fish sauce
2 garlic cloves, crushed
60ml sweet chilli sauce
4 tbsp chopped fresh mint
6 frenched racks lamb, 4 cutlets on each
20ml groundnut (peanut) oil

chilli-mint sauce
2 heaped tbsp grated palm sugar*
40ml groundnut (peanut) oil
60ml seasoned rice vinegar
1 lime, juiced, zested
20ml fish sauce
2 small red chillies, deseeded and
   thinly sliced
2 spring onions, sliced on the diagonal
120g fresh mint, roughly chopped

Combine the fish sauce, garlic, chilli sauce and mint and rub over the lamb. Refrigerate for 30 minutes.

Preheat the oven to 200°C/400°F/gas mark 6.

Heat the oil over a medium-high heat, then cook the lamb racks for 1-2 minutes each side. Transfer to a baking tray and roast for 6-8 minutes until cooked through. Allow to rest for 5 minutes. (This will be rare; cook a little longer if you prefer it well-done.)

To make the chilli-mint sauce, combine all the sauce ingredients and serve immediately over the lamb rack with a sweet-potato *rösti* or mashed potato.

*Available from Asian supermarkets.

Serves 6

easy lamb **pilaf**

20ml olive oil
1 onion, sliced
2 tsp *ras el hanout** (moroccan seasoning)
500g lamb fillet, diced
250g basmati rice
500ml beef or vegetable stock
50g dried apricots, chopped
1 x 400g can chickpeas, rinsed, drained
1 heaped tbsp toasted pine nuts*
mint leaves, tzatziki and flatbread, to serve

Heat the oil in a deep, non-stick frying pan over a medium heat. Add the onion and cook for 5 minutes or until just turning golden. Add the spice and cook for a few seconds, then add the lamb and stir for 2-3 minutes, until the meat is browned.

Stir in the rice, then add the stock and bring to the boil. Reduce the heat to low and simmer for 10 minutes, or until the rice is tender and most of the stock is absorbed.

Stir in the apricots, chickpeas and pine nuts. Garnish with mint and serve with tzatziki and flatbread.

**Ras el hanout* is available from Middle Eastern shops. Ready-toasted pine nuts are available from supermarkets.

Serves 4-6

moroccan lamb with chickpea salad

2 heaped tbsp *ras el hanout**
  (*see* p. 148)
60ml extra-virgin olive oil
2 x 250g lamb loins, trimmed
1 x 400g can chickpeas, rinsed
  and drained
1 red onion, thinly sliced
2 tomatoes, seeds removed, chopped
2 heaped tbsp chopped
  coriander leaves
2 heaped tbsp chopped mint leaves
4 tbsp tahini*
1 garlic clove, crushed
60ml lemon juice, plus wedges to serve
pitta bread, to serve
100g-120g baby (micro) salad leaves*

In a bowl, mix the spice-mix powder with 20ml of the olive oil. Brush over the lamb and set aside.

Place the chickpeas, onion, tomato, coriander and mint in a bowl. In a separate bowl, whisk the tahini, garlic, lemon juice and 40ml of water until you have a loose dressing. Toss the salad with the dressing.

Heat a chargrill pan or barbecue to a medium-high heat and cook the lamb for 2-3 minutes each side, until lightly charred but still rare inside. Set aside to rest for 2-3 minutes in a warm place.

Lightly toast the pitta bread on the grill pan. Serve the lamb, sliced, with the salad, grilled pitta bread, baby salad leaves and lemon wedges on the side.

*Tahini is available from the health-food aisle of your supermarket. Baby or micro salad leaves are available from farmers' markets and selected greengrocers. If unavailable, garnish with extra mint and coriander.

Serves 4

5 OF THE BEST
beef

beef **fillet** with **wild** **mushroom** vinaigrette

125ml extra-virgin olive oil
2 garlic cloves, crushed
2 heaped tbsp chopped
   thyme leaves
1.2kg fillet of beef, well-trimmed
40ml red-wine vinegar
2 tsp dijon mustard
30g unsalted butter
250g mixed wild mushrooms
   (such as oyster, enoki, shimeji
   and chanterelles)
100ml beef stock
2 heaped tbsp snipped chives
watercress, to serve

Mix 40ml of the oil in a dish with the garlic and thyme. Add the beef fillet and coat in the mixture. Cover and refrigerate for 2-3 hours.

Place the remaining oil, vinegar and mustard in a bowl and whisk to combine. Season with salt and pepper.

Preheat the oven to 190°C/375°F/gas mark 5.

Heat the butter in a large frying pan over a high heat, add the mushrooms and cook 2-3 minutes, until just wilted. Add the stock and heat through, then add the mixture to the bowl with the vinaigrette. Add half the chives and set aside.

Return the pan to the heat and brown the beef all over, then place it in a roasting pan and roast for 20 minutes for rare, or until cooked to your liking. Remove and set aside to rest for 10 minutes.

To serve, place a thick slice of beef on each plate. Add any roasting-pan juices to the mushroom vinaigrette, then spoon over the beef and garnish with chives. Serve with watercress.

Serves 6-8

steak & kidney tartlets

40ml olive oil
400g chuck steak,
   trimmed, diced
100g onion, finely chopped
4 lamb kidneys, core and sinew
   removed, meat chopped
100g button
   mushrooms, quartered
25g plain flour
1 tsp marmite
400ml good-quality beef stock
200ml guinness
1 bay leaf
4 thin slices prosciutto
chopped flat-leaf parsley,
   to garnish

for the tart shell
150g plain flour
75g wholemeal flour
1 tsp chopped thyme
125g unsalted butter, chilled

To make the tart shells, place the flours in a food processor with the thyme, butter and a pinch of salt. Process until the mixture resembles fine breadcrumbs. Add 60ml of chilled water and process until the mixture comes together to form a smooth ball. Wrap in plastic wrap and refrigerate for 30 minutes.

Divide the pastry into quarters and form into 4 small balls. Roll each ball out on a lightly floured board, then use to line four 10cm x 3cm loose-bottomed fluted tart pans. Refrigerate for 30 minutes.

Preheat the oven to 190°C/375°F/gas mark 5.

Line the pastry cases with non-stick baking paper, fill with rice or pastry weights and bake for 10 minutes. Remove the paper and weights and return to the oven for 5 minutes, or until golden and crisp. Set aside. (These tart shells can be made one day in advance and kept in a sealed container.)

Heat the oil in a saucepan over high heat and cook the beef in two batches until brown and sealed. Transfer to a plate; set aside.

Add a little more oil if necessary and cook the onions over a low heat for about 5 minutes, or until softened. Add the kidneys and mushrooms and fry over a medium heat, stirring, for a further 2 minutes. Return the steak to the pan with the flour and cook for 1 minute. Stir in the Marmite, stock, Guinness and bay leaf. Bring to the boil over a high heat, then reduce the heat to low, cover and cook for 1 hour. Remove the lid and allow the liquid to reduce for about 10 minutes until quite thick.

Reduce the oven to 180°C/350°F/gas mark 4.

Meanwhile, line a baking tray with baking paper. Place the slices of prosciutto on the tray and bake for 5 minutes, or until crisp. Place the pastry cases on a separate baking sheet and reheat for 5 minutes.

To serve, put a warm pastry case on each plate and spoon in the steak and kidney filling. Sprinkle with parsley and place a crisp shard of prosciutto on the side. Accompany with mashed potato.

Serves 4

cubed **steak** with **chilli** & **coriander** dressing

20ml soy sauce
1 tsp ground szechuan pepper*
2.5cm piece ginger, grated
1 garlic clove, crushed
125ml safflower or sunflower oil
6 x 200g eye-fillet steaks, well-trimmed
250ml seasoned rice vinegar
175g caster sugar
1 tsp salt
1 long red chilli, seeds removed, chopped
4 tbsp finely chopped coriander
crème fraîche, thai chilli jam*, jasmine
   rice and snowpea sprouts, to serve

Mix the soy, pepper, ginger, garlic and oil in a shallow dish, add the steaks, cover and marinate in the fridge for up to 2 hours.

Stir the vinegar and sugar over a low heat to dissolve the sugar. Simmer for 2 minutes, then stir in the salt. Cool, then add the chilli and coriander. Set aside.

Heat a chargrill or barbecue to a high heat. Cook the steaks (in batches if necessary) for 1-2 minutes each side. Rest the steaks for 1-2 minutes, then cut into cubes.

Arrange the cubes in the shape of original steaks on plates. Drizzle with the dressing. Serve with crème fraîche, chilli jam and rice, and garnish with the sprouts.

*Available from Asian and selected supermarkets.

Serves 6

rare **roast beef** & **horseradish** galette

40ml bottled horseradish,
  or 80ml horseradish cream
250ml sour cream
1 sheet frozen butter puff
  pastry, thawed, cut
  into 4 squares
1 egg, beaten
500g piece rib-eye fillet,
  well-trimmed
30ml olive oil
125ml red wine
2 bunches thin asparagus, halved

Preheat the oven to 200°C/400°F/gas mark 6.

Combine the horseradish and sour cream and put in the fridge.

Place the pastry on a lightly greased baking tray, brush with
the egg and bake for 10 minutes, until golden. Set aside.

Season the beef with salt and pepper. Heat the oil in an ovenproof
frying pan over a high heat, then add the beef and seal on all
sides. Transfer to the oven for 12 minutes, then remove from the
pan and rest in a warm place before slicing. Return the pan to a
high heat, add the wine and stir 1-2 minutes until reduced slightly.

Cook the asparagus in boiling salted water for 1 minute and drain.
Split the pastry lids from their bottoms, and place the bottoms on
plates. Top each with beef, asparagus and horseradish. Put the
pastry lids on top and drizzle with the pan juices.

Serves 4

fillet of beef **bourguignonne**

80ml extra-virgin olive oil
1 x 1.5kg fillet of beef, well-trimmed
120g mild pancetta, diced
2 garlic cloves, crushed
500ml red wine
10g dried porcini mushrooms,
    soaked in 60ml warm water
500ml good-quality beef stock
1 heaped tbsp tomato paste
2 sprigs thyme, chopped
2 bay leaves
bunch of baby carrots, ends trimmed,
    blanched (halved if large)
12 shallots, blanched, halved
1 heaped tbsp plain flour
4 tbsp butter
200g small portobello or shiitake
    mushrooms, sliced
finely chopped parsley, to garnish

Heat half the oil in an ovenproof casserole over a high heat, then add the beef fillet and brown on all sides. Transfer to a plate and set aside.

Heat the remaining oil in the casserole over a medium heat. Add the pancetta and fry for 5 minutes, or until it starts to crisp. Transfer to a plate lined with paper towels.

Drain all but 2 tablespoons of fat from the casserole, then add the garlic and cook for a few seconds. Add the red wine and porcini mushrooms with their soaking liquid, stock, tomato paste and herbs. Season with salt and pepper, then bring to the boil.

Reduce the heat to low and simmer for 15 minutes, then strain the sauce, discarding all the solids and return the sauce to the casserole to cook for 5 minutes, or until slightly reduced. Place the meat in the sauce with the carrots and onions and simmer over a low heat for 10 minutes for rare meat (a little longer if you prefer your meat more well-done).

Transfer the meat to a platter, cover loosely with foil and set aside to rest.

Use a fork to mash the flour with 1 tablespoon of butter, then gently whisk into the sauce and cook over a low heat for 2 minutes. Meanwhile, sauté the mushrooms with the remaining butter over a medium heat in a separate pan, then add to the sauce. Taste for seasoning.

Place the fillet on a serving platter surrounded with the vegetables. Pour a little sauce over the beef fillet, sprinkle with parsley, and serve the remaining sauce separately.

Serves 6

5 OF THE BEST
stir-fries

stir-fried noodles with **beef** & **greens**

1 tsp schezuan peppercorns* or black peppercorns, crushed
$\frac{1}{2}$ tsp chinese five spice powder
40ml groundnut (peanut) oil
500g beef eye fillet, trimmed
40ml dark soy sauce
$\frac{1}{2}$ tsp sugar
40ml oyster sauce, plus extra to drizzle
20ml sesame oil
2 garlic cloves, crushed
1 red chilli, deseeded, finely chopped
2 tsp grated ginger
6 spring onions, sliced on the diagonal
450g thin hokkien noodles
150g baby spinach leaves
80g roasted cashew nuts

Preheat the oven to 190°C/375°F/gas mark 5.

Combine the peppercorns, five-spice and half the groundnut oil. Roll the beef fillet in the mixture.

Heat a non-stick pan over a high heat, add the beef and fry until brown all over. Transfer to a baking tray and roast in the oven for 8 minutes. Remove from the oven and set aside.

Combine the soy, sugar, oyster sauce and sesame oil in a bowl. Heat the remaining groundnut oil in a wok over a medium-high heat. Add the garlic, chilli and ginger and cook for 30 seconds. Add the spring onions and noodles and cook for 1 minute. Add the spinach and sauce mixture and cook until well-coated. Add the cashews.

Slice the beef and serve on the noodles. Drizzle with the oyster sauce.

* Available from Asian supermarkets.

Serves 4

spicy stir-fried **aubergine**

40ml vegetable oil
20ml sesame oil
400g aubergine, cut into 2cm pieces
1 small red pepper, deseeded and chopped
1 onion, sliced
4 garlic cloves, finely chopped
2 tsp grated fresh ginger
150g fresh shiitake mushrooms
1 x 110g can bamboo shoots
300ml vegetable stock
80ml shaohsing rice wine*
2 heaped tbsp chopped fresh coriander
steamed rice, to serve

for the stir-fry bean sauce
60ml black bean sauce
40ml oyster sauce
20ml soy sauce
60ml tomato ketchup
2 tsp cornflour

To make the sauce, put the black bean, oyster, soy sauce and ketchup in a bowl and mix together. Combine the cornflour with a little cold water, then add to the other ingredients. Set aside.

Heat the oils in a wok over high heat, then add the aubergine, pepper and onion and stir-fry for 2-3 minutes. Add the garlic, ginger, mushrooms and bamboo shoots and stir-fry for 1 minute.

Add the stock and shaohsing rice wine, bring to the boil, then add the sauce. Keep stir-frying for about 2-3 minutes, or until the mixture thickens.

Serve over steamed rice garnished with chopped coriander.

*Rice wine is available from Asian supermarkets; if you can't find it, use dry sherry.

Serves 4

stir-fried rice with chilli tuna

4 cups cooked long-grain rice
40ml olive oil
8 bacon rashers, rind removed, diced
1 garlic clove, crushed
120g fresh or frozen peas
1 x 210g can tuna in chilli
  oil*, drained
300g spring onions, finely sliced,
  plus extra to serve
60ml light soy sauce,
  plus extra to serve

Heat the oil in a wok over a high heat, add the bacon and fry until crisp. Remove and drain on kitchen paper.

Add the rice and garlic to the wok, stir-fry for 1 minute, then add the peas, tuna, spring onions, cooked bacon and soy sauce. Stir-fry quickly until heated through.

Serve with extra soy sauce and spring onions.

* If you can't find tuna in chilli oil, add 1 finely chopped chilli, seeds removed, with the rice and garlic.

Serves 4

thai-style pork &
hokkien noodle stir-fry

450g thin fresh hokkien noodles*
40ml vegetable oil
350g pork fillet, thinly sliced
1 onion, thinly sliced
1 carrot, cut into thin strips
1 small red chilli, deseeded, chopped
4 garlic cloves, crushed
2 heaped tbsp thai red curry paste
40ml fish sauce
1 heaped tbsp brown sugar
20ml lime juice
4 spring onions, sliced on the diagonal
coriander leaves, to garnish

Rinse the noodles under cold water, separate and drain in a colander. Set aside.

Heat 20ml of the oil in a wok over a high heat. Fry the pork in batches for 2-3 minutes, or until cooked through, then set aside.

Heat the remaining oil and add the onion and carrot and stir-fry for 1 minute. Add the chilli, garlic and curry paste, then stir-fry for a further minute.

Return the pork to the wok and add the fish sauce, sugar, lime juice and noodles. Cook until heated through, then add half the spring onions and use the remainder to garnish with the coriander.

* Available from Asian supermarkets.

Serves 4

stir-fry chicken with pesto

40ml olive oil
4 small skinless chicken breast fillets
   (about 160g each), thinly sliced
1 red pepper, cut into thin strips
225g portobello mushrooms, sliced
200g baby spinach leaves
1 punnet cherry tomatoes, halved
150ml single cream
2 heaped tbsp good-quality pesto
small basil leaves, to garnish
steamed rice, to serve

Heat 20ml of the oil in a large non-stick frying pan over a high heat and cook the chicken for 5-6 minutes, until golden and cooked through. Remove and set aside.

Add the remaining oil to the pan along with the pepper and mushrooms, and cook, stirring, for 1-2 minutes. Add the spinach and tomato, and cook until the spinach just wilts. Return the chicken to the pan.

Combine the cream and pesto in a small bowl, then add to the pan and cook until just heated through.

Sprinkle with basil and serve with rice.

Serves 4

5 OF THE BEST
casseroles

fruity **beef** casserole

40ml olive oil
1kg lean stewing beef, diced
2 onions, thinly sliced
2 carrots, peeled, sliced
2 garlic cloves, crushed
1 heaped tbsp tomato paste
1 heaped tbsp plain flour
½ tsp chilli powder
1 lemon, zested, plus 1 tbsp
   (20ml) juice
375ml beef stock
160g plum jam
chopped flat-leaf parsley, to garnish
creamy mashed potato, to serve

Preheat the oven to 170°C/325°F/gas mark 3.

Heat the olive oil in a large ovenproof casserole dish over a medium heat. Add the beef in batches and cook until browned all over. Transfer to a plate and set aside to rest.

Add the onion to the pan and cook, stirring, for 1-2 minutes until softened. Add the carrot, garlic, tomato paste, flour and chilli powder. Stir to combine and cook for a further minute.

Add the lemon rind and lemon juice, beef, stock and plum jam (the liquid needs to just cover the meat, so add a little water if necessary). Season well with salt and pepper and bring to the boil, then place in the preheated oven and cook for 2 hours until the beef is tender.

Garnish with the parsley and serve with some creamy mashed potato.

Serves 4

venison casserole

1.5kg venison shoulder, diced
60ml olive oil
150g *speck**, chopped
2 onions, peeled and chopped
2 carrots, peeled and diced
1 garlic clove, crushed
500ml strong stock (beef or game)
bouquet garni
2 heaped tbsp redcurrant jelly
60ml single cream
1 x 210g jar marinated chanterelle
   mushrooms*, drained, or 300g
   sautéed mixed wild mushrooms
chopped parsley, to garnish

for the marinade
350ml good-quality red wine
6 juniper berries, lightly crushed
1 onion, sliced
60ml brandy
60ml olive oil
2 bay leaves
2 thyme sprigs

To make the marinade, put all the ingredients in a large non-metallic bowl. Add the venison, stir to combine, then cover and place in the fridge for 24 hours.

Preheat the oven to 150°C/300°F/gas mark 2.

Heat 40ml of the olive oil in large flameproof casserole dish over a medium-high heat, then add the *Speck* and fry until crispy. Remove and drain on paper towels.

Remove the venison with a slotted spoon, reserving the marinade mixture. Return the casserole dish to the heat and fry the meat in batches over a high heat until browned. Remove the meat and set aside.

Add the remaining oil, then fry the onions and carrots over a medium heat for 1-2 minutes, or until beginning to soften. Stir through the garlic, then add the reserved marinade to the pan along with the meat and *Speck*. Pour in enough stock to just cover the meat, then add the bouquet garni. Cover and cook in oven for 2 hours, or until the meat is tender.

Remove from the oven, stir in the redcurrant jelly, cream and mushrooms, then cover and cook for a further 15 minutes. Garnish with chopped parsley and serve with noodles or mashed potato.

Speck, a kind of German cured ham, is available from delis. Use prosciutto if not available. Marinated chanterelles are available from good delicatessens.

Serves 6-8

polenta with **sausage** casserole

1 onion, roughly chopped
1 carrot, roughly chopped
1 large celery stick, roughly chopped
2 garlic cloves
40ml olive oil
12 baby chipolata sausages
200g portobello
    mushrooms, quartered
150ml red wine
1 x 400g can chopped tomatoes
2 heaped tbsp sun-dried tomato pesto
1/2 tsp sugar
1 heaped tbsp chopped fresh oregano,
    or 1 tsp dried oregano
2 tbsp basil leaves, plus extra
    to garnish
200g instant polenta
40g butter
100g grated parmesan

Place the onion, carrot, celery and garlic in a food processor. Process until finely chopped. Set aside.

Heat the oil in a large frying pan over a medium heat. When hot, add the sausages and cook for 2-3 minutes, until golden brown. Transfer to a plate and set aside.

Add the vegetables to the pan and cook over a medium heat for about 5 minutes, until softened. Add the mushrooms and cook for a further minute. Add the wine, tomatoes, pesto, sugar and oregano. Season well with salt and pepper. Bring to the boil, then reduce the heat to low, cover and cook for 15 minutes.

Remove the lid, add the sausages and cook for 15 minutes, or until the sauce is thick. Stir in the basil.

Meanwhile, bring 1 litre of water to the boil. Reduce the heat to low and add the polenta in a slow, steady stream. Cook for 6-7 minutes, stirring constantly.

Remove from the heat and stir in the butter and half the Parmesan. Season well.

Place some polenta on each plate, top with the casserole and garnish with the basil. Serve with the remaining Parmesan.

Serves 4

chorizo & bean stew

700g new potatoes, quartered
60ml olive oil
1 red onion, peeled, chopped
500g *chorizo* sausage, sliced*
4 garlic cloves, crushed
1 tsp dried chilli flakes
1 x 400g can butter-beans, rinsed
   and drained
1 x 410g can diced tomatoes
2 fresh bay leaves
150ml beef or chicken stock
5 tbsp chopped flat-leaf parsley

Place the potatoes in a large saucepan of cold, salted water. Bring to the boil and simmer for 10 minutes, or until just tender. Remove from the heat. Drain.

Heat the oil in the same pan. Add the onion and cook for 3-4 minutes, until just softened. Add the *chorizo* and cook until it starts to turn golden. Transfer the mixture to a plate.

Add the garlic and chilli to the pan. Cook for a few seconds, then add the potatoes, butter-beans, tomatoes, bay leaves, and the *chorizo* mixture. Pour in the stock, bring to the boil, then reduce the heat to low and simmer for 10 minutes. Stir in the parsley and serve with crusty bread.

**Chorizo* is a spicy Spanish sausage available from good delicatessens and some supermarkets.

Serves 4

lamb tagine

1.5kg shoulder lamb, diced
1 large spanish onion, grated
2 garlic cloves, crushed
1 bunch coriander, leaves chopped
1 cinnamon stick
1 tsp each ground cumin, ground
   ginger, paprika, saffron threads
120ml olive oil
1 large piece orange peel
1 x 800g can chopped tomatoes
2 heaped tbsp tomato paste
375ml beef stock
1 bay leaf
30g butter, diced
40ml honey
1 x 240g can chickpeas, drained
   and rinsed
75g green olives
chopped mint, to garnish

Combine the lamb, onion, garlic, coriander, spices, oil and 1 teaspoon of salt in a bowl. Cover and refrigerate overnight.

Preheat oven to 160°C/325°F/gas mark 3. Heat a non-stick frying pan, add the lamb in batches and fry until lightly browned all over. As the meat is cooked, place it in a tagine or casserole dish. Add the orange peel.

Drain the tomatoes, reserving the juice, then set tomatoes aside. Combine the juice with the tomato paste, then add to the meat along with the stock and bay leaf. Cover and cook in oven for 1½ hours.

Use a slotted spoon to transfer the meat to a plate. Place the dish over a high heat (if using a tagine, you'll need to transfer the liquid to a frying pan). Add the diced tomatoes and butter and reduce for 2 minutes, then add the honey, chickpeas, olives and meat. Cook, stirring, for 1-2 minutes. Garnish with mint to serve.

Serves 8

5 OF THE BEST
curries

thai chicken & asparagus curry

40ml sunflower oil
700g chicken breast fillets,
    cut into 2cm cubes
1 large onion, finely chopped
2 garlic cloves, crushed
1 lemon-grass stem, outer leaves
    removed, quartered lengthways
5 tbsp green curry paste
300ml coconut milk
250ml chicken stock
2 heaped tbsp green
    peppercorns*, drained
2 kaffir lime leaves*
1 bunch thin asparagus, woody
    ends trimmed, halved
fish sauce, to season
coriander leaves, steamed jasmine
    rice and lime wedges, to serve

Heat the oil in a wok over a high heat. Stir-fry the chicken in batches until golden all over. Transfer to a bowl and set aside.

Return the wok to the heat (you may need to add a little oil). Add the onion, garlic and lemon grass and stir-fry for 1 minute. Add the curry paste and cook, stirring, for a further minute.

Return the chicken to the wok and add the coconut milk, stock, peppercorns and kaffir lime leaves, then bring to the boil. Reduce the heat to medium and simmer for 2 minutes. Add the asparagus and cook for a further 2 minutes, or until bright green. Season to taste with the fish sauce.

Serve the curry, garnished with coriander, with jasmine rice and lime wedges.

*Green peppercorns are available from supermarkets. Kaffir lime leaves are available from Asian shops and greengrocers.

Serves 4

low-fat **kofta** curry

500g lean beef mince
1 garlic clove, crushed
1 tsp grated fresh ginger
1 tsp ground chilli
1 tsp garam masala
2 onions, roughly grated
5 tbsp korma curry paste
20ml sunflower oil
200ml beef stock
1 x 400g can crushed tomatoes
175ml low-fat evaporated milk
40ml lemon juice
60g frozen peas
steamed rice, to serve
chopped fresh coriander, to garnish

Combine the beef, garlic, ginger, chilli, garam masala, half the onion and 1 tablespoon of curry paste. Season with salt and pepper, then form into walnut-sized balls.

Heat the oil in a non-stick frying pan over a medium heat, add the kofta balls and cook in batches until lightly browned. Transfer to a plate.

Add the remaining onion to the pan and cook over a very low heat until soft and lightly golden. Add the remaining curry paste, stock and tomatoes and cook over a medium heat, stirring, for 5 minutes.

Add the milk and lemon juice. Return the kofta to the pan and simmer over a low heat for 15 minutes.

Add the peas and cook for 2 minutes. Serve with rice and garnish with coriander.

Serves 6

lamb & aubergine curry

1 large aubergine, cut in half
  lengthways, sliced
40ml sunflower oil
1 large onion, thinly sliced
300g lamb fillet, sinew trimmed, diced
3 tsp thai green curry paste
2 kaffir lime leaves
400ml coconut milk
100g baby french beans
40ml light soy sauce
40ml fish sauce
50g baby spinach leaves
steamed jasmine rice and
  lime wedges, to serve

Sprinkle the aubergine with salt and set aside for 30 minutes to degorge. Rinse and squeeze dry in a tea towel.

Heat the oil in a wok. When hot, add the aubergine and fry over a high heat for 1-2 minutes, until golden. Drain on paper towels.

Add the onion to the wok (you may need to add a little oil) and fry for 1-2 minutes. Add the lamb and cook for 1 minute, then add the curry paste and lime leaves. Cook over high heat for a few seconds.

Return the aubergine to the wok and add the coconut milk and beans. Bring to the boil. Add the soy sauce, fish sauce and spinach, stirring to wilt the spinach.

Serve with the rice and limes.

Serves 4

easy **masaman** curry

20ml groundnut (peanut) oil
1 onion, chopped
3-4 tbsp thai masaman curry paste*
600g diced topside or chuck beef
1 heaped tbsp plain flour
2 kaffir lime leaves
500ml beef stock
150ml coconut milk
1 carrot, peeled, roughly chopped
1 large potato, peeled, cut into chunks
125g mange-tout
20ml fish sauce
1 heaped tbsp chopped
   fresh coriander
steamed jasmine rice, to serve

Heat the oil in a saucepan over a medium heat. Add the onion and cook, stirring, for 2 minutes. Add the curry paste and cook for a few seconds to release the flavours, then add the beef and cook for 1-2 minutes, stirring to prevent it from catching.

Add the flour, lime leaves, stock, coconut milk and carrot and stir to combine. Bring to the boil, then reduce the heat to low and cook, covered, for 40 minutes.

Add the potatoes and cook, partially covered, for 30 minutes.

Add the mange-tout, fish sauce and coriander and cook for 1 minute. Serve with jasmine rice.

*Available from selected supermarkets and Asian delis.

Serves 6-8

chicken & coconut curry

120ml soy sauce
2 heaped tbsp ground cumin
4 tbsp mild curry paste
1 tbsp ground turmeric
2 garlic cloves, crushed
5 tbsp sweet chilli sauce
3 sticks lemon grass, finely chopped
4 (130g each) single chicken breasts,
    cut into 2cm pieces
6$\frac{1}{2}$ tbsp crunchy peanut butter
300ml coconut milk
2 fresh kaffir lime leaves*
chopped fresh coriander, to garnish
coconut rice, to serve

Combine the soy, cumin, curry paste, turmeric, garlic, sweet chilli sauce and lemon grass in a bowl. Add the chicken and stir well. Cover and refrigerate overnight (or during the day) to marinate.

Place the marinated chicken, peanut butter, coconut milk and lime leaves in a saucepan and cook over a low heat, stirring occasionally, for 20-25 minutes, or until the chicken is cooked through.

Garnish with extra coriander and serve with coconut rice (*see* recipe p. 146).

*Kaffir lime leaves are available from Asian shops and greengrocers.

Serves 4

little **pear** tartlets

6 small pears
1 lemon, halved
220g caster sugar
1 vanilla bean, split,
    seeds scraped
3 sheets butter puff
    pastry, thawed
200g block marzipan, sliced
1 egg, lightly beaten
icing sugar, to dust
double cream, to serve

Peel the pears and rub the surface with the cut side of a lemon half. Place the sugar in a saucepan with 500ml of water, and the vanilla pod and seeds. Stir over a low heat to dissolve the sugar, then add the pears, bring to a simmer, and poach for 6-8 minutes, or until just softened (time will depend on ripeness of pears). Remove and cool slightly.

Preheat the oven to 180°C/350°F/gas mark 4. Line a large baking tray with baking paper.

Halve the pears lengthwise and remove the cores, leaving the stalks attached. Cut lengthwise slices in each half almost to the top, leaving the narrow end intact to keep the shape. Use your palm to gently flatten the pear halves and fan out the slices.

Cut the pastry into 12 circles slightly larger than the pears and lay the circles on the baking tray. Place a slice of marzipan in the centre of each circle and top with a pear. Lightly score the pastry around the edge of the pears, not cutting completely through, then brush the pastry with the egg. Bake for 20-25 minutes, until puffed.

Preheat the grill to high. Remove the tray from the oven and dust the tartlets with the icing sugar, then place them under the grill for 1 minute, or until tinged golden. Watch carefully so they do not burn. Alternatively, use a blowtorch.

Place on a platter decorated with seasonal leaves. Drizzle with double cream and serve two tartlets per person .

Serves 6

mascarpone & cherry tarts

225g plain flour
5 tbsp icing sugar, sifted,
  plus a little extra to dust
180g chilled unsalted butter,
  roughly chopped
100g amarena fabbri cherries
  in syrup*
300ml whipping cream
200g mascarpone cheese
1/2 tsp vanilla extract
toasted flaked almonds

Put the flour, half the icing sugar and the butter in a food processor and process until the mixture resembles fine crumbs. Add 30ml of chilled water, then process until the mixture comes together to form a smooth ball. Wrap in plastic wrap and refrigerate for 30 minutes.

Lightly grease eight 10cm loose-bottomed tart pans. Roll out the dough on a lightly floured work surface, then use it to line the pans. Cover and refrigerate for a further 15 minutes.

Preheat the oven to 190°C/375°F/gas mark 5.

Line each tart case with baking paper and fill with uncooked rice or pastry weights. Blind bake for 10 minutes, remove the paper and beans or weights, then bake for a further 5 minutes. Remove from the oven and allow to cool.

Drain the cherries, reserving the syrup. In a bowl, beat the cream until thick, then add the mascarpone, the remaining icing sugar and vanilla, and beat until combined.

Fill the tart shells with the cream mixture. Dust the rims with icing sugar and put the cherries on top of the tarts. To serve, drizzle with the reserved syrup, sprinkle with the flaked almonds.

*Amarena fabbri cherries are are small, dark-red and slightly sour, and are preserved in sugar syrup. Available from delicatessens or selected gourmet food stores. Any leftover cherries may be kept in the fridge for up to 2 months.

Makes 8

strawberry amaretti tarts

150g amaretti biscuits
80g unsalted butter, melted, cooled
200g mascarpone
2 heaped tbsp icing sugar,
  plus extra to dust
½ tsp vanilla extract
150g diced strawberries
20ml *vincotto** or balsamic vinegar

Preheat the oven to 170°C/325°F/gas mark 3. Lightly grease 4 round loose-bottomed tart pans (2cm deep, 8cm in diameter.)

Crush the biscuits in a food processor, combine with the melted butter and press the mixture into the base and sides of the pans. Bake for 10 minutes, then allow to cool slightly. Remove the cases from the pans and set aside to cool completely.

Whip the mascarpone with 1½ tablespoons of icing sugar and the vanilla. Toss the strawberries with the remaining icing sugar and *vincotto*.

Fill the tarts with the mascarpone, then pile on the strawberries, dust with icing sugar and drizzle with any remaining *vincotto*.

**Vincotto* is cooked grape-must vinegar and is available from gourmet food stores.

Makes 4

tarte **tatin**

6 golden delicious or royal
  gala apples
40ml lemon juice
200g vanilla sugar
30g unsalted butter, cubed
250g puff pastry
double cream or
  ice-cream, to serve

Peel and core the apples and cut into quarters. Place in a large bowl and toss in the lemon juice and 100g vanilla sugar.

Put the remaining sugar and 40ml of water in an ovenproof frying pan or 25cm tarte tatin pan over a low heat, stirring to dissolve the sugar. Increase the heat to medium and cook for about 5 minutes, until the sugar caramelizes and is a light-golden brown. Add the apple, cut-side up, and dot with the butter. Keeping the heat very low, cook for a further 5-6 minutes. Remove from the heat and set aside to cool.

Preheat the oven to 190°C/375°F/gas mark 5. Roll out the pastry and cut into a circle slightly larger than the pan. Put the pastry over the apples, tucking any excess underneath. Put the pan on a baking tray and bake for 35 minutes, until the pastry is golden. Remove from the oven and rest in the pan for 10 minutes. Carefully turn the tart upside down onto a large plate. Serve with cream or ice-cream.

Serves 4-6

pear & ginger tart

250g ginger-nut biscuits
125g unsalted butter, melted
175g caster sugar
3 firm pears
450ml whipping cream
20ml poire william* (optional)
1 heaped tbsp icing
    sugar, sifted
60ml prepared good-quality
    caramel sauce, to serve
6 almonds (skin on),
    thinly sliced

Crush the biscuits in a food processor and mix with the melted butter. Use the biscuit mixture to line the base and sides of a 25cm x 11cm rectangular, loose-bottomed tart pan, pressing in firmly. Cover and refrigerate for 30 minutes.

Place the sugar in a saucepan, add 500ml of water and stir over a low heat to dissolve the sugar.

Peel the pears and add them to the pan, topping up with enough water to cover. Bring to the boil, reduce the heat to low, cover and poach for 10 minutes, or until the fruit is cooked (this will depend on the ripeness of the pears). Allow the fruit to cool in the syrup.

When ready to serve, remove the pears (the poaching liquid can be frozen and used for poaching fruit). Drain the pears well, patting dry with paper towel, and slice thinly, discarding the cores. Lay the slices over the biscuit base.

Beat together the cream, Poire William and icing sugar, spread over the pears and drizzle with the caramel sauce. Garnish with sliced almonds.

*Poire William is a French pear liqueur, available from selected off-licences.

Serves 4

5 OF THE BEST
cold desserts

buttermilk puddings with candied kumquats

Begin this recipe the day before.

300ml single cream
125g caster sugar
1 vanilla bean, split,
    seeds scraped
3 sheets (15g) leaf
    gelatine or 3 tsp
    powdered gelatine
600ml buttermilk

for the candied kumquats
75g caster sugar
200g kumquats, quartered
2 tbsp cointreau

Put half the cream in a saucepan over a low heat along with the sugar, and vanilla bean and seeds. Stir until the sugar dissolves.

If you are using leaf gelatine, soak the leaves in cold water for a few minutes, then drain and add to the warm cream mixture. If using powdered gelatine, sprinkle over the warm cream mixture, then whisk gently to dissolve.

Strain the mixture through a sieve into a clean bowl, then gradually add the buttermilk (make sure to shake the carton well beforehand to distribute the solids).

Whip the remaining cream and fold it into the mixture, then pour into six 150ml dariole (timbale) moulds. Refrigerate overnight.

Meanwhile, to make the candied kumquats, dissolve the sugar in a saucepan with 200ml water. Boil for 2 minutes, then add the kumquats, reduce the heat to low and simmer until they start to soften. Cook for 15-20 minutes, or until the mixture is jammy, then stir in the Cointreau.

Dip the base of the pudding moulds in warm water, then turn out onto serving plates. Serve with the kumquats on top.

Serves 6

cassata trifle

200g sponge fingers (*savoiardi*)
150ml *vin santo** or other
   dessert wine
450g fresh or frozen raspberries,
   plus extra to serve
500g fresh ricotta cheese
50g icing sugar
600ml whipping cream
25g mixed glacé fruits, chopped
100g grated dark chocolate

Break half the *savoiardi* into 2cm pieces and spread them in a
1.5-litre glass serving dish. Drizzle with half the *vin santo* and
top with one-third of the raspberries.

Process the ricotta, icing sugar and half the cream in a food
processor until smooth, then spread over the sponge base.
Top with the remaining raspberries. Break the remaining
savoiardi over the top and sprinkle with the remaining wine.

Whip the remaining cream until soft peaks form and fold in the
fruit and two-thirds of the chocolate. Spread over the sponge
layer. Top with the remaining grated chocolate and a few extra
raspberries to finish.

*Vin santo is available from selected wine merchants.

Serves 8

eton mess

225g raspberries,
    fresh or frozen
55g caster sugar
450g strawberries, hulled
    and quartered
150ml double cream
150ml thick greek yoghurt
4 (10g each) meringue
    nests, crumbled

Put the raspberries and sugar in a saucepan over a very low heat for 5 minutes until the juices start to flow, then leave to cool. Transfer to a food processor and purée until smooth. Pass through a sieve, discarding the solids.

Put the strawberries in a bowl together with the purée, cream, yoghurt and the meringue.

Fold everything together until just combined, then spoon into four glasses and serve immediately.

Makes 4

yoghurt & berry brulée

600g thick greek yoghurt
1 punnet (120g) raspberries
1 punnet (120g) blueberries
120g strawberries, halved
1-2 small peaches, sliced
220g caster sugar

Put the yoghurt in a serving dish, scatter the berries over the top, then add the peaches.

Put the sugar in a heavy-based saucepan along with 310ml of water and stir over a low heat until the sugar has dissolved. Increase the heat to medium and continue to cook until the mixture becomes a golden caramel colour.

Quickly pour the hot toffee over the fruits. Serve as soon as possible. Some of the toffee will melt into the yoghurt, and some will turn into crisp shards.

Serves 8

little pavs with tropical fruits & passion-fruit sauce

4 egg whites
490g caster sugar
½ tsp white vinegar
½ tsp vanilla extract
2 tsp cornflour
6 passion fruit
200ml whipping
   cream, whipped
sliced banana, kiwi fruit,
   pineapple and
   blueberries, to serve

Preheat the oven to 180°C/350°F/gas mark 4. Whisk the egg whites until stiff. Gradually add 270g of the sugar and whisk until glossy. Whisk in the vinegar, vanilla and cornflour.

Draw six 10cm circles on a piece of non-stick baking paper and place on a baking tray. Mound the mixture into the circles and bake for 5 minutes. Reduce the oven to 110°C/225°F/gas mark ¼ for 25 minutes. Turn off the oven and leave for 2-3 hours to dry out.

Put the remaining sugar in a pan with 250ml water and stir over a low heat until dissolved. Increase the heat to medium-high and cook for 5 minutes to reduce by half. Put the passion-fruit pulp in a food processor and whiz for a few seconds; add to the sugar syrup. Return to the heat and then cook for 5 minutes over a low heat. Set aside to cool.

Put a pavlova on each plate, add a dollop of cream and slices of fruit and drizzle with the passion-fruit sauce.

Makes 6

5 OF THE BEST
cheesecake

white chocolate cheesecakes with mango & strawberries

100g wholemeal biscuits
30g unsalted butter, melted
75g good-quality
   white chocolate
250g cream cheese
110g caster sugar
1 egg
60ml single cream
strawberries, hulled and halved,
   mango slices and pulp of
   1 passion fruit, to serve

Preheat the oven to 160°C/325°F/gas mark 3.

Grease two 10cm x 4cm individual springform moulds.

Place the biscuits in a food processor and process until the mixture resembles fine breadcrumbs, then add the melted butter and process again. Divide the mixture between the moulds, pressing down well. Refrigerate while you make the topping.

Melt the chocolate in a bowl over a pan of gently simmering water (don't let the bowl touch the water), then set aside for a few minutes to cool.

Clean the processor, add the cooled chocolate, cream cheese, sugar, egg and cream, then process until smooth. Spread the filling on top of the biscuit base.

Bake for 20 minutes, turn off the heat and allow the cakes to cool in the oven, then refrigerate until firm. Serve, topped with the strawberries, mango slices and passion-fruit pulp.

Makes 2 cheesecakes

banoffee cheesecake

70g unsalted butter, melted
3 tsp powdered gelatine
100g wholemeal biscuits, broken
2 eggs, separated
75g caster sugar
225g mascarpone
1 vanilla bean, split, seeds removed
300ml double cream, whipped
2 bananas, sliced
50g flaked almonds, roasted

for the toffee sauce
150ml whipping cream
75g unsalted butter
150g brown sugar
1 tsp vanilla extract

Use a little of the melted butter to brush the base and sides of a 20cm springform pan. Line the base with baking paper. Dissolve the gelatine in 2 tablespoons of hot water. Set aside.

Crush the biscuits in a food processor. Combine the remaining butter with the biscuit crumbs and press into the base of the pan.

Put the egg yolks, two-thirds of the sugar, the mascarpone and the seeds from the vanilla bean in an electric mixer and beat until pale. Fold in the gelatine and whipped cream.

Beat the egg whites and remaining sugar in a bowl until stiff peaks form, then fold into the cheese mixture. Spoon over the base, then refrigerate overnight.

To make the toffee sauce, put all the ingredients in a pan over a low heat, stirring to dissolve the sugar. Increase the heat to high and cook, stirring, for a further 2 minutes. Set aside to cool, then refrigerate for 2-3 hours before serving.

To serve, arrange the banana slices on top of the cake, drizzle with the sauce and sprinkle with almonds.

Serves 8-10

new york cheesecake

200g nice biscuits
75g unsalted
    butter, melted
800g cream cheese
190g caster sugar
4 eggs
3 egg yolks
3 tsp vanilla extract
30ml lemon juice
300ml sour cream
good-quality cocoa
    powder, to dust

Preheat the oven to 180°C/350°F/gas mark 4.

Grease a 23cm round springform pan. Place 2 layers of aluminium foil on the outside of the pan (this prevents water seeping into the pan while cooking in the water bath).

Crush the biscuits in a food processor. Combine the melted butter with the biscuit crumbs and press into the base of the pan.

Put the cream cheese, 170g caster sugar, eggs, egg yolks, 2 teaspoons of the vanilla extract and the lemon juice in a food processor. Process until smooth, then pour over the biscuit base. Place the cheesecake in a large roasting pan and pour boiling water into the roasting pan to come halfway up the sides of the springform pan. Bake in the oven for 1 hour.

Beat together the sour cream, the remaining sugar and vanilla and pour over the cake. Return to the oven for a further 10 minutes. Remove from the oven and set aside in the pan to cool, then refrigerate for 4 hours. Serve dusted with cocoa powder.

Serves 10-12

lemon, lime & ginger cheesecakes

125g ginger-nut biscuits
60g unsalted butter, melted
45g lemon jelly crystals (such as Quik-jel)
40ml lime juice
200g cream cheese
110g caster sugar
½ tsp vanilla extract
200ml evaporated milk, well-chilled
tropical fruits (such as kiwi fruit, lychees and passion fruit), to serve

Preheat the oven to 120°C/250°F/gas mark ½.

Crush the biscuits in a food processor, then add the butter and mix until combined. Use the crumb mixture to line the base of six greased 8cm x 3cm loose-bottomed tart pans. Bake in the oven for 10 minutes. Set aside to cool.

Dissolve the jelly crystals in 80ml boiling water. Add the lime juice and set aside to cool slightly.

Beat the cream cheese, sugar and vanilla extract together until combined, then add the jelly mixture. Whip the evaporated milk until it has thickened, then fold into the cheese mixture. Spoon into the biscuit-lined pans and refrigerate overnight.

Serve with a mix of your favourite tropical fruits.

Makes 6

rosewater cheesecake with strawberries

Begin this recipe the day before.

250g digestive biscuits, crushed
100g unsalted butter, melted
4 gelatine leaves or 1 sachet
  gelatine crystals
500g cream cheese
110g caster sugar
3 tsp rosewater
300ml whipping cream
160g rose-petal* or strawberry jam
250g punnet strawberries, sliced

Grease a 22cm springform cake pan. Combine the biscuits and butter, then press into the base of the pan.

Place the gelatine in a bowl of cold water, stand for 5 minutes, then drain and squeeze out any excess water. Return the gelatine to the bowl and pour over 60ml boiling water. Whisk with a fork until smooth, then cool slightly.

Whiz the cream cheese and sugar in a food processor until smooth. Add the cooled gelatine and rosewater. Process to combine.

Whip the cream with electric beaters until slightly thickened. Add the cheese mixture, beat until smooth, then pour over the crumb base. Cover loosely and chill overnight.

When ready to serve, warm the jam in the microwave for 30 seconds, then stir in the strawberries. Slice the cheesecake and top with the strawberry mixture.

*Rose-petal jam is available from Middle Eastern and gourmet food shops.

Serves 8

vanilla gelato with vanilla-strawberry sauce

500ml milk
2 vanilla beans, split
6 egg yolks
200g caster sugar
500ml single cream, chilled
1 tsp vanilla extract

for the vanilla-strawberry sauce
55g caster sugar
250g punnet strawberries
160g strawberry jam
$1/2$ tsp vanilla extract

Pour the milk in a pan. Scrape in the seeds from vanilla beans and add beans, too. Bring to a boil, then remove from the heat and set aside for 30 minutes to infuse.

Meanwhile, place the egg yolks and sugar in the bowl of an electric mixer and beat on high for 3 minutes, until pale. Add the infused milk and stir to combine. Return to the pan and cook over a low heat, stirring constantly, for 3-4 minutes until slightly thickened. Remove from the heat and set aside to cool slightly, then stir in the cream. Add the vanilla extract, stir to combine, then refrigerate until cooled completely.

Strain the mixture into a shallow container, discarding the beans, and freeze until frozen at the edges. Remove from the freezer and beat with an electric beater. Pour back into the container and refreeze. Repeat 2 or 3 times. (Alternatively, use an ice-cream machine.)

To make the vanilla-strawberry sauce, put the sugar and 125ml water in a saucepan over a low heat for 1-2 minutes, stirring to dissolve the sugar. Add the strawberries, jam and vanilla extract and stir over a low heat for 1 minute. Set aside to cool slightly, then blend to a smooth purée. Refrigerate for 30 minutes before serving over the *gelato*.

Serves 4-6

nougat semifreddo with blueberry compote

3 eggs, separated
60ml honey
300g mascarpone
120g nougat, roughly chopped

for the blueberry compote
500g blueberries
275ml dry marsala
40g caster sugar
1 cinnamon stick
1 vanilla bean, seeds scraped
1 tsp arrowroot

Preheat the oven to 180°C/350°F/gas mark 4.

To make the compote, put the blueberries, marsala, sugar, cinnamon and vanilla seeds and bean in a large baking dish. Bake uncovered for 40 minutes.

Remove and strain into a pan, reserving the berries. Combine the arrowroot with 20-45ml cold water and add to the juices in the pan. Cook, stirring constantly, over a low heat until it thickens slightly. Set aside to cool, then cover and refrigerate. Remove the vanilla and cinnamon just before serving.

Put the egg yolks and honey in the bowl of an electric mixer and beat the mixture until pale. Add the mascarpone and beat to combine. Fold in the nougat and set aside.

Beat the egg whites until stiff, then fold in until combined.

Line a 25cm x 10cm terrine with plastic wrap and fill with the mixture, pushing down well. Freeze until firm. Refrigerate for 30 minutes before serving.

Serve with compote and reserved berries.

Serves 8-10

baci ice-cream

6 egg yolks
125g caster sugar
900ml double cream,
    plus extra to serve
150g good-quality
    dark chocolate
40g good-quality cocoa
    powder, sifted
250g nutella
20ml-40ml tbsp
    hazelnut syrup*
2-3 baci chocolates,
    quartered, to garnish

Whisk the egg yolks with the sugar until light. Pour 600ml of the cream in a saucepan and heat over a medium heat until it reaches scalding point. Add to the egg-yolk mixture and beat well.

Melt the chocolate in a heatproof bowl over a pan of simmering water. Cool slightly, then stir the cream mixture into the chocolate. Add the cocoa, put in a saucepan and cook over a low heat until thickened. Cool a bit, whisk in the Nutella and syrup, then cool further. Whip the remaining cream and fold into the chocolate mixture.

Lightly grease a 25cm x 11cm terrine and line with plastic wrap. Fill the terrine with the ice-cream and smooth the top. Freeze overnight or until firm. Remove from the freezer, dip the terrine base in warm water, then gently ease out onto a serving platter; discard the plastic wrap. To serve, garnish with the extra cream and the chopped chocolates.

*Hazelnut syrup is available from selected gourmet food stores or sold in cafés as a coffee flavouring.

Serves 8-12

iced **raspberry** parfait

350g raspberries
120g caster sugar
40ml framboise or
    semi-sweet sherry
2 egg whites
450ml double cream
55g icing sugar

Set aside 50g of the raspberries to garnish. Put the remaining raspberries in a food processor along with the caster sugar and framboise. Process until you have a purée, then pass this through a sieve to remove any seeds.

Whisk the egg whites until stiff peaks form, then, in a separate large bowl, whip the cream and icing sugar until the mixture has thickened. Fold the egg whites into the cream along with the raspberry purée.

Place the mixture in a plastic container or into six 125ml soufflé dishes and freeze until firm.

Transfer to the fridge 10 minutes before serving to soften slightly. Serve garnished with the remaining raspberries.

Serves 6

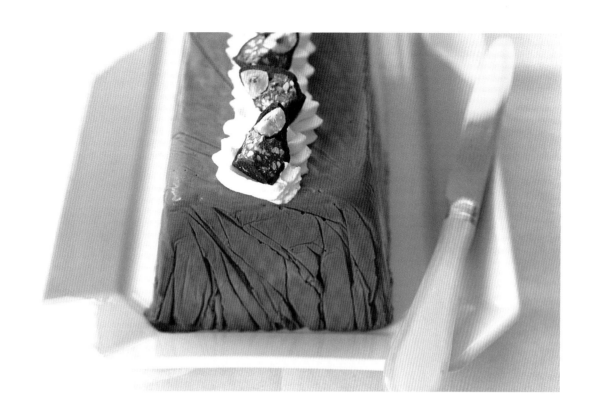

lemon & mascarpone sorbetto

2 lemons
250g caster sugar
500g mascarpone
poached blueberries or fresh
    fruit compote, to serve

Remove the lemon zest in strips, making sure you leave behind any white pith. Juice the lemons.

Put the sugar and 450ml of water in a pan over a low heat. Stir until the sugar dissolves, then add the lemon zest and juice. Simmer for 3 minutes, cool, then strain (discard the zest).

Place the mascarpone in a bowl and slowly whisk in the cooled lemon syrup. Churn in an ice-cream machine following manufacturer's directions. Alternatively, pour the mixture into a shallow container and freeze for 2-3 hours until frozen at the edges. Transfer to a food processor and pulse several times until smooth. Pour back into container and re-freeze, repeating the process once more, then allow to freeze completely.

Serve with poached or fresh fruit.

Serves 4

5OF THE BEST
hot puddings

raspberry & white chocolate waffle pudding

480g (about 14) waffles
300g raspberries (fresh are best, but frozen are fine)
200g good-quality white chocolate, chopped
55g caster sugar
1 heaped tbsp plain flour
3 eggs
1 tsp grated lemon rind
1 tsp vanilla extract
500ml double cream
2 heaped tbsp icing sugar, to dust

Preheat the oven to 170°C/325°F/gas mark 3.

Butter a medium ovenproof dish. Cut the waffles into 2cm cubes and put half in the dish, topped by half the raspberries, then half the chocolate. Repeat the layers.

Whisk together the sugar, flour, eggs, rind, vanilla and cream. Pour over the waffles and set aside for 10 minutes.

Bake in the oven for 35 minutes, until golden.

Dust with icing sugar and serve with cream or ice-cream.

Serves 6-8

caramel apple pudding

5 large golden delicious or granny smith
   apples, peeled, cored, sliced 1cm thick
250g plain flour
2 tsp baking powder
250g caster sugar
200ml milk
150g unsalted butter, melted
2 eggs, beaten
200g light muscovado sugar
   or light brown sugar
115g golden syrup
icing sugar and double cream, to serve

Preheat the oven to 180°C/350°F/ gas mark 4.

Lightly butter a 2.5-litre baking dish. Place the apples in the prepared dish.

Sift the flour and baking powder into the bowl of an electric mixer, add the caster sugar, milk, butter and egg, then beat until pale. Spread the mixture over the apples.

Place the muscovado or brown sugar, golden syrup and 300ml water in a saucepan. Stir over a medium heat until the sugar dissolves, then bring to the boil without stirring. Pour over the pudding batter, then bake for 30–35 minutes or until the top is golden.

Dust with icing sugar and serve with cream.

Serves 6-8

warm brownie puddings
with chocolate sauce

120g good-quality dark chocolate
125g unsalted butter
4 eggs
220g caster sugar
20ml frangelico or amaretto
75g plain flour
$^1/_2$ tsp baking powder
50g good-quality cocoa powder
thick cream to serve

for the chocolate sauce
125g good-quality dark chocolate
185ml single cream

Preheat the oven to 180°C/350°F/gas mark 4 and butter four 1-cup ramekins or ovenproof cups.

Place 120g of chocolate and the butter in a heatproof bowl over simmering water (don't let the bowl touch the water), stirring until smooth. Remove from the heat and cool slightly.

Using electric beaters, beat the eggs until foamy, then add the sugar and beat until pale and thick. Gradually add the chocolate mixture, then stir in the Frangelico or amaretto. Sift the flour, baking powder and cocoa, then fold into the mixture. Pour into the prepared ramekins or cups and bake for 25 minutes.

For the sauce, place the ingredients in a heatproof bowl and melt as above until a thick sauce forms.

Serve the puddings in ramekins or cups, topped with warm sauce and cream.

Makes 4

malted chocolate pudding
with mars bar custard

125g unsalted butter, softened
125g caster sugar
2 eggs
125g plain flour
50g malted milk powder
1 tsp baking powder
40-60ml cold milk
1 heaped tbsp cocoa powder
600ml carton custard
65g mars bar, cut into
   small pieces
20g chopped walnuts, lightly
   toasted, to garnish

Grease a 1-litre pudding basin. Beat the butter and sugar until pale and fluffy. Add the eggs one at a time, beating well. Sift in the flour, malted milk and baking powder. Add enough milk for a dropping consistency.

Put half the mixture in a separate bowl and sift in the cocoa. Put alternate spoonfuls of each mixture into the pudding basin. Gently swirl them together with a skewer.

Cover with foil and tie with kitchen string. Put an upturned plate in a large saucepan and stand the pudding on top. Pour boiling water to halfway up the sides of the pudding basin. Bring to a boil, then reduce the heat to low. Cover and steam for 2 hours.

Just before serving, put the custard and Mars bar in a pan over a low heat. Stir until the bar has melted. Turn out the pudding, serve with the Mars bar custard, and garnish with the walnuts.

Serves 4-6

orange bread & butter pudding

400g good-quality fresh white
  bread, crusts removed
150g butter, melted
225g orange marmalade*
3 oranges, peeled, segmented,
  plus extra 1 orange,
  rind grated
3 eggs
500ml single cream
100g caster sugar
4 tbsp demerara sugar

Preheat the oven to 180°C/350°F/gas mark 4. Butter a 16cm x 32cm x 5cm baking dish.

Cut the bread into rough chunks and place in a large bowl and pour the butter on top.

Heat the marmalade in a saucepan over a low heat until warm, then pour over the bread. Add the orange segments and stir carefully. Tip the mixture into the prepared dish.

Beat together the orange rind, eggs, cream and caster sugar, then pour over the bread. Sprinkle with demerara sugar and bake in the oven for 35-40 minutes, until golden.

* We used Duchy Originals Organic Blood Orange Marmalade, available from delicatessens and some supermarkets.

Serves 4-6

5 OF THE BEST
pikelets & pancakes

blueberry pancakes with mango butter & cream

150g self-raising flour
1 tsp bicarbonate of soda
40g caster sugar
1 egg
350ml buttermilk
15g butter, melted
    plus extra to brush
2 punnets (240g total) blueberries
fresh mango slices, mango butter
    and double cream, to serve
icing sugar, to dust

for the mango butter
600g (3-4 mangoes) mango flesh
115ml lemon juice
115ml orange juice
800g caster sugar

Sift the flour and bicarbonate of soda into a large bowl and add the sugar. In a separate bowl, beat the egg, buttermilk and melted butter together, then mix with the dry ingredients until you have a smooth batter. Add half the blueberries.

Heat a large non-stick frying pan over a medium heat and brush with butter. Place a dessertspoon of batter for each pancake into the frying pan and cook in batches, 3 or 4 at a time, for 1-2 minutes or until bubbles start to form on the surface. Turn the pancakes over and cook the other side for a further minute. Remove from the pan and keep warm while you cook the rest.

Stack 3 or 4 pancakes on each plate and top with the remaining blueberries, fresh mango, mango butter (recipe follows) and double cream. Dust with icing sugar.

Serves 8

To make the mango butter, put the mango flesh into a saucepan along with the lemon and orange juices. Bring to the boil, then simmer over a low heat for 10-15 minutes, or until no liquid is left.

Purée the mixture, strain into a bowl, then return to pan. Add the sugar and stir over a low heat until dissolved.

Reduce the heat to very low and simmer for about 30 minutes, stirring from time to time, until thick. Spoon into sterilised jars, cover and seal. Store for 3-4 weeks in the fridge.

Makes 375ml

blintzes with **sour cream** & cherries

175g cottage cheese
100g cream cheese
1 egg yolk
½ tsp vanilla extract
1 heaped tbsp caster sugar
finely grated zest of ½ lemon
20g unsalted butter, melted
12 crêpes (*see* p. 231)
sour cream, to serve

for the cherry sauce
1 x 425g can pitted cherries
   in syrup
75g caster sugar
2–3 tbsp kirsch (cherry
   brandy), optional
1 tsp arrowroot

To make the sauce, put the cherries, syrup and sugar in a pan . Stir over a medium heat until the sugar dissolves, then add the Kirsch. Mix the arrowroot with 20ml of cold water, stirring until smooth. Add a little warm juice to the arrowroot mixture, then tip it all into the juice. Cook, stirring, for 1-2 minutes until the sauce thickens. Set aside to cool.

Preheat oven to 180°C/350°F/gas mark 4 and brush a 20cm x 25cm baking dish with melted butter. Put the cheeses, egg yolk, vanilla, sugar and zest in a food processor and blend until smooth.

Place a generous tablespoon of cheese mixture in the centre of each crêpe. Fold in the sides, then bottom and top to form a parcel. Put the blintzes fold-side down into a dish (you may need to overlap slightly). Brush the tops with the remaining butter. (At this stage you can cover and chill until ready to cook). Bake for 15 minutes.

To serve, place two blintzes on each plate and top with the sauce and sour cream.

Serves 6

orange hotcakes

300g self-raising flour, sifted
2 heaped tbsp caster sugar
2 eggs
250ml buttermilk
3 oranges
40g butter, melted
thick greek yoghurt, to serve

Put the flour and sugar in a bowl and stir to combine.

In a separate bowl, beat together the eggs, buttermilk and the rind and juice of 1 orange. Beat together the wet and dry ingredients until combined and smooth. Set aside. Peel and remove the pith from the remaining oranges and cut into thin half-slices.

Put a non-stick frying pan over a medium heat and brush with a little butter. Drop 2–3 tablespoons of batter in the pan to form a hotcake and cook for 1 minute, or until small holes appear on the surface. Flip and cook for 1-2 minutes on the other side. Keep warm while cooking remaining hotcakes, brushing the pan with a little butter when needed.

Put 2 or 3 hotcakes on each plate, add the orange slices and a dollop of yoghurt. Dust with icing sugar, if desired.

Serves 4-6

coconut pancakes with palm sugar syrup

500g dark palm sugar*, grated
1 vanilla bean, split, seeds scraped
150g plain flour
1 tsp baking powder
1 heaped tbsp caster sugar
40g desiccated coconut
2 eggs, separated
125ml milk
125ml coconut milk
25g unsalted butter, melted,
 plus extra to brush
3-4 bananas, sliced lengthways

To make the syrup, put the palm sugar in a pan together with the vanilla pod and seeds and 2 cups of water. Bring to the boil, then reduce the heat and simmer for 15 minutes, without stirring, until reduced by half. Strain and cool, then refrigerate until needed.

Sift the dry ingredients into a bowl and add the coconut. Beat the egg yolks, milk, coconut milk and melted butter together in a separate bowl, then whisk into the dry ingredients.

In a clean bowl, beat the egg whites with a pinch of salt until soft peaks form, then use a metal spoon to carefully fold them into the batter.

Heat a non-stick frypan over a medium heat and brush with a little extra butter. Drop double tablespoonfuls of the mixture into the pan 2-3cm apart and cook for 1-2 minutes, until golden. Flip and cook for 1 minute on other side. Transfer to a baking tray loosely covered with foil and keep warm in a low oven while you use remaining batter.

Allow 2-3 pancakes per person along with 1 banana. Drizzle with syrup to serve.

*Available from Asian food stores.

Serves 3-4

crêpes with **walnut cream** & **butterscotch** sauce

100g light brown sugar
80g unsalted
    butter, cubed
425ml whipping cream
2 tbsp icing sugar
20ml brandy
2 tsp coffee and
    chicory essence*
4 tbsp chopped
    toasted walnuts
12 crêpes
    (*see* recipe below)

for the crêpes
150g plain flour
1 tsp caster sugar
240ml milk
2 eggs

Place the sugar in a pan over a medium-low heat. Add the butter and 125ml of the cream. Stir until the sugar dissolves, then increase the heat to medium. Cook, without stirring, for 5 minutes. Cool and set aside.

Whip the remaining 300ml cream until thick. Stir in the icing sugar, brandy, essence and 2 tbsp nuts.

Take a cooled crêpe and spread one quarter with a heaped tablespoonful of cream. Fold in half, then in half again to enclose the filling. Repeat with the remaining crêpes.

Allow 2 crêpes per person. Sprinkle with the remaining nuts and drizzle with butterscotch sauce to serve.

*From the coffee aisle in most supermarkets. Use coffee essence if unavailable.

Serves 6

basic crêpe recipe
Put the ingredients in a food processor or blender with a pinch of salt. Blend until smooth, then strain into a jug. Cover and set aside to rest for 30 minutes at room temperature.

Dip a piece of paper towel in melted butter and use to brush base of a 16cm non-stick crêpe pan or frying pan over a medium heat. When hot, pour in just enough batter to cover the base. Tilt the pan so that the batter covers the base in a thin film and pour any excess back into the jug. Cook for about 1 minute, until the underside is golden, then use a metal spatula to flip it. Cook the other side for just under a minute, until golden. Transfer to a plate and cover with foil to keep warm. Repeat with the remaining mixture, stacking the crêpes on the plate as you go.

Note To freeze cooked crêpes, stack them with a sheet of greaseproof paper between each. Wrap the stack in plastic wrap and freeze for up to 3 months. Defrost for 1 hour at room temperature

Makes 12

5 OF THE BEST
big cakes

chocolate **cherry** liqueur cake

175g good-quality
  dark chocolate
80ml cherry liqueur
100ml strong black espresso
75g caster sugar
3 eggs, separated
100g unsalted butter,
  melted and cooled
50g ground almonds
50g plain flour, sifted
425g can pitted black cherries,
  drained, with 60ml
  juice reserved

**for the chocolate-cherry
icing and syrup**
100g good-quality dark
  chocolate
60ml reserved cherry juice
80ml cherry liqueur*
100g unsalted butter, cubed
2 tsp arrowroot

Preheat the oven to 180°C/350°F/gas mark 4. Grease and line the base of a 20cm springform cake pan.

Place the chocolate, cherry liqueur and espresso in a bowl over a saucepan of gently simmering water until melted. Set aside to cool.

Reserve 1 heaped tablespoon of the caster sugar. Place the remaining sugar and egg yolks in the bowl of an electric mixer and beat until pale and light. Add the cooled melted butter and almond meal and beat until combined. Combine with the chocolate mixture.

Beat the egg whites until stiff. Add the reserved caster sugar and continue to beat until thick and glossy. Gradually fold the egg whites, alternating with the flour, into the cake mixture.

Reserve half the cherries, then fold the remaining half into the cake mixture and pour into the lined pan. Bake in the oven for 30 minutes, or until a skewer inserted into the centre comes out clean. Turn out onto a wire rack to cool.

To make the chocolate-cherry icing and syrup, put the chocolate, 2 tablespoons of the cherry juice and 2½ tablespoons of the cherry liqueur in a bowl over a pan of simmering water. Once the chocolate has melted, gradually add the butter, beating until combined. Remove from the heat and continue beating until cool and smooth. Set aside the icing at room temperature.

To make the syrup, combine the arrowroot, remaining cherry juice and reserved cherries and liqueur in a saucepan over a low heat and stir for about 1-2 minutes until thickened and syrupy. Set aside to cool.

To serve, spread the top of the cooled cake with the chocolate-cherry icing. Cut the cake into wedges and serve drizzled with the cherry syrup.

Serves 4-6

strawberry vacherin

175g whole blanched almonds
5 egg whites
225g caster sugar
110g unsalted butter,
  melted and cooled
70g plain flour, sifted
300ml double cream, whipped
150g pure icing sugar,
  plus extra to dust
1 tsp vanilla extract
100g toblerone chocolate
250g punnet strawberries

Preheat the oven to 120°C/250°F/gas mark ½.

Lightly roast the almonds in the oven for about 20 minutes. Transfer to a food processor and process to a fine powder.

Cut three 20cm circles from non-stick baking paper. Grease one side of the circles and place them on baking trays, greased-side up.

Beat together the egg whites and half the caster sugar in the bowl of an electric mixer until stiff. Add the ground almond and remaining sugar, and stir to combine. Gently fold in the butter and flour. Spread onto the baking-paper circles to 1cm thick and bake for 50 minutes, then peel off the paper and set aside to cool.

Beat together the cream, icing sugar and vanilla extract in a bowl until thick. Set aside.

Melt the Toblerone in a bowl over a pan of gently simmering water. Set aside to cool slightly.

Place one meringue round on a plate, spread with half the Toblerone and top with a third of the cream mixture. Repeat, then top with the third meringue and pile the remaining cream mixture on top. Cut the strawberries lengthways into quarters and arrange on top. Dust with the icing sugar.

Serves 8-10

semolina **shortbread** with caramelized apples

120g unsalted butter, softened,
  plus extra to grease
55g granulated sugar
150g plain flour
50g fine semolina
½ tsp vanilla extract
200g mascarpone
1 heaped tbsp icing sugar

for the caramelized apples
40g unsalted butter
3 golden delicious apples,
  peeled, core removed, sliced
20ml lemon juice
20ml amaretto (or brandy)
90g caster sugar

Preheat the oven to 140°C/275°F/gas mark 1. Brush a 36cm x 11cm loose-bottomed fluted tart pan with butter.

Beat the butter and sugar together for 2 minutes, until pale. Slowly start adding the flour and semolina, the vanilla and a pinch of salt until all are incorporated. Carefully press into the prepared pan and use a fork to prick the mixture. Bake for 40 minutes, or until cooked but still pale.

To make the apples, melt the butter in a large pan over a medium heat. Add the apples and cook until golden. Sprinkle with the lemon juice, amaretto and sugar. Reduce the heat to low and cook until golden and caramelized. Set aside to cool.

To serve, whip the mascarpone with the icing sugar. Cut the shortbread into six wedges and spread each with some mascarpone. Top with the apples, drizzle with the pan juices.

Serves 6

plum cake with plum syrup

1kg dark plums
125ml red wine
1 cinnamon stick
1 piece orange peel
300g caster sugar
150g unsalted butter,
    softened, and extra
    for greasing
3 eggs
170ml sour cream
350g plain flour, sifted
25g baking powder
120g pecans
300ml double cream,
    lightly whipped

Put the plums, wine, cinnamon, orange peel and 120g sugar in a large saucepan. Pour in enough water to just cover the fruit, then put over a low heat, stirring to dissolve the sugar. Poach for 10 minutes, or until the fruit is just soft. Transfer the plums to a bowl and return the liquid to a high heat. Bring to a boil; leave until only 250ml of liquid remains. Pour into a serving jug and refrigerate until ready to serve.

Preheat the oven to 170°C/325°F/gas mark 3. Grease and line the base of a 26cm springform pan.

Stone and chop the plums; keep 150g in reserve. Cream the butter and remaining sugar until pale and add the eggs, one at a time. Stir in the sour cream; fold in the flour, baking powder and nuts. Carefully fold in the plums. Spoon into the pan and bake for 50-60 minutes, or until a skewer inserted into the centre comes out clean. Set aside to cool in the pan.

Fold the reserved plums through the whipped cream and serve the cake drizzled with sauce and with the plum-flavoured cream.

Serves 8-10

orange syrup cake

250g unsalted butter, softened
495g caster sugar
4 large oranges
3 eggs
240g crème fraîche
2 heaped tbsp
   thin-cut marmalade
265g cups plain flour
1 tsp bicarbonate soda
1 tsp baking powder

Preheat the oven to 170°C/325°F/gas mark 3. Grease and lightly flour a 2-litre bundt or tube pan.*

Place the butter and 225g of sugar in an electric mixer and beat at a high speed until light and fluffy. Grate the rind from two oranges and add to the mixture. Squeeze the juice from these oranges and set aside.

Add the eggs, one at a time, to the mixture, beating well after each addition. Add the crème fraîche and marmalade, beating slowly until combined. Sift the flour, bicarbonate soda and baking powder into the mixture, then use a metal spoon to carefully fold in the dry ingredients until combined.

Pour the batter into the prepared pan, smoothing the top. Bake for 50-60 minutes, or until a skewer inserted into the centre comes out clean. Set aside to cool, then turn out onto a wire rack placed over a tray.

To prepare the syrup, cut the remaining oranges into thin slices and set aside. Put the reserved orange juice, remaining sugar and 250ml of water in a saucepan over a low heat, stirring until the sugar has dissolved. Add the orange slices and simmer for 10-15 minutes, until the slices are transparent. Lay these out on a wire rack and continue cooking syrup until well-reduced.

While the cake is still warm, use a skewer to make small holes over the surface, then drizzle with the syrup. Place the orange slices on top of the cake, twisting them to form a decorative pattern.

*Bundt tins are similar to Savarin ring moulds, and are now available from selected kitchenware shops.

Serves 8-10

5 OF THE BEST
small cakes

carrot cakes

440g brown sugar
375ml vegetable oil
4 eggs, beaten
480g grated carrot
  (about 4 medium)
450g plain flour
2 tsp baking powder
2 tsp baking soda
2 tsp ground cinnamon
1 tsp ground ginger
80ml milk
1/2 tsp salt

for the coconut icing & decoration
200g icing sugar
80-100ml coconut cream
1 large carrot, peeled
110g caster sugar

Preheat the oven to 180°C/350°F/gas mark 4.

Put all the cake ingredients in a large bowl and use a wooden spoon to mix until it becomes a smooth batter.

Pour into lightly greased muffin pans, or a greased and lined 24cm cake tin. Bake in the oven for 25 minutes (or 1 hour for a large cake), or until a skewer comes out clean.

Meanwhile, to make the coconut icing and decoration, combine the icing sugar with the coconut cream until you have a smooth mixture. Set aside.

Use a zester to make long shreds from the carrot.

Put the sugar and 125ml of water in a pan over a low heat. Stir to dissolve the sugar, then bring to the boil and cook for 2 minutes. Add the carrot and cook for a further 5 minutes, until it's sticky and caramelized. Drain on paper towels.

Drizzle the icing over the cooled cakes, then place some caramelized carrot on top.

Makes 12 muffin-size cakes, or 1 24cm cake which serves 6-8

mini **chocolate** cakes

200g unsalted butter, chopped
200g good-quality cooking
  chocolate, (70% cocoa
  solids), chopped
2 heaped tbsp instant
  coffee powder
1 tsp vanilla extract
3 eggs
220g caster sugar
115g self-raising flour, sifted
30g cocoa powder
fresh raspberries, to garnish

for the ganache
125ml single cream
150g good-quality cooking
  chocolate (70% cocoa
  solids), chopped

Preheat the oven to 160°C/325°F/gas mark 3. Grease and line the base of a 20cm x 30cm lamington pan*.

Put the butter, chocolate, coffee, vanilla and 60ml water in a saucepan. Stir over a low heat until smooth, then allow to cool.

Beat the eggs and sugar with an electric mixer until pale and thick. Stir in the chocolate mixture, then fold in the flour and cocoa powder.

Pour into the pan and bake for 35-40 minutes, or until a skewer inserted into the centre comes out clean. Remove from the oven and cool slightly in pan. Turn out onto a board and use a 6cm pastry cutter to cut 12 rounds.

To make the ganache, heat the cream to scalding point in a small saucepan. Put the chocolate in a heatproof bowl and pour the cream over the top, stirring until the chocolate has melted.

Pour a little ganache over each round of cake, allowing it to drip down the sides. Garnish with fresh raspberries.

*A lamington pan is about 3cm deep, so any cake tin with roughly these same measurements will do.

Makes 12

lemon friands with lemon curd & blueberries

You can make the friands a day ahead. Simply reheat for 30 seconds in a microwave. You will need six medium brioche or 12 friand pans for this recipe.

180g unsalted butter, plus extra to grease
250g icing sugar, plus extra to dust
80g plain flour
125g ground almonds
2 lemons, zested
5 egg whites
20ml lemon juice
1 tsp vanilla extract
blueberries and whipped cream, to serve

for the lemon curd
4 lemons, washed and dried
4 eggs
340g caster sugar
250g unsalted butter
1 heaped tbsp cornflour

Preheat the oven to 180°C/350°F/gas mark 4.

Lightly grease your choice of pans with a little butter.

Place the butter in a pan over a low heat. When it has melted, cook it for 3-4 minutes until you start to see flecks of brown appear. Set aside to cool.

Sift the icing sugar and flour into a bowl and stir in the almond meal and lemon zest.

In a clean bowl, whisk the egg whites until frothy (do not over-whisk as you just need to loosen, not aerate, them). Add to the dry ingredients along with the melted butter, lemon juice and vanilla. Use a metal spoon to combine, then fill the moulds three-quarters full and place on a baking tray. Bake in the oven for 25 minutes, until light golden (a skewer inserted into the centre should come out clean).

Meanwhile, to make the lemon curd, finely grate the lemon zest. Use your hand to roll the lemons over a flat surface several times (this helps extract all the juice), then juice them.

Place all the ingredients in a heavy-based saucepan and stir to combine. Cook over a low heat, stirring constantly, for 10 minutes, or until thick. Pour into a bowl and cover the surface with plastic wrap to prevent a skin from forming. If you wish to keep for longer, pour into a sterilized jar and seal while still hot. Keep refrigerated.

To serve, spoon some lemon curd over the top of each friand, and top with blueberries and a dollop of whipped cream.

Makes 6 (or 12, depending on the pan)

strawberry lamingtons

8 eggs, separated, plus 2 yolks
190g caster sugar
80g plain flour
40g cornflour
40g butter, melted, cooled
1 tsp vanilla extract
100g desiccated coconut

for the strawberry icing
30g unsalted butter
5 tbsp plus 1 tsp strawberry
  jelly crystals
300g icing sugar, sifted

Preheat oven to 180°C/350°F/gas mark 4. Grease and line a 30cm x 18cm lamington pan*.

Place 10 egg yolks and 90g sugar in a bowl and beat until pale. Transfer to a large bowl. Sift the flours together, then fold into the yolk mixture.

Fold in the butter. Beat the egg whites with the remaining sugar and vanilla; fold half into the yolk mixture, then fold in the other half. Spread the mixture into the pan and bake for 15 minutes. Remove from the oven and cover with a tea towel.

To make the icing, put the butter and jelly crystals in a bowl, add 250ml boiling water and stir to dissolve the butter. Sift in the icing sugar; whisk until smooth. Set aside to cool. Cut the sponge into 12 squares, dip in the icing, then roll in the coconut.

*A lamington pan is about 3cm deep, so any cake tin with roughly these same measurements will do.

Makes about 12

mini gingerbreads

200g unsalted butter
160g dark brown sugar
60ml golden syrup
2 eggs
165ml milk
300g self-raising flour, sifted
2 tsp ground ginger
4 tbsp chopped
  crystallized ginger
150g icing sugar, sifted
2-3 tsp lemon juice

Preheat the oven to 170°C/325°F/gas mark 3. Grease and line the base of six 185ml mini loaf pans.

Stir the butter, brown sugar and golden syrup in a saucepan over a low heat until melted. Cool for 10 minutes. Whisk the eggs and milk in a bowl to combine, then stir into the cooled sugar mixture.

Put the flour, ground ginger and a pinch of salt in a separate large bowl. Use a wooden spoon to beat in the egg mixture and 1 tablespoon crystallized ginger. Divide the batter among loaf pans, then bake for 35-40 minutes, until a skewer inserted in centre comes out clean. Cool slightly in the pans, then turn out onto a rack to cool completely.

In a bowl, stir the icing sugar and 2 teaspoons lemon juice until smooth, adding a little more juice if needed. Drizzle the icing over the cakes. Decorate with the remaining chopped ginger.

Makes 6

picture credits

Cold Starters pages 8-15
Prosciutto Wraps Photography: Ben Dearnley, Styling: Julz Beresford | Simple Antipasto Photography: Ben Dearnley, Styling: Louise Pickford | Sushi Timbales Photography: Mark Roper, Styling: Julz Beresford Tuna-stuffed Peppers Photography: Ian Wallace, Styling: Louise Pickford | Tuna Sashimi Photography: Mark Roper, Styling: Julz Beresford

Chilled Soups pages 16-23
Herb Garden Soup Photography: Ian Wallace, Styling: Michelle Noerianto | Cucumber Soup with Garlic Prawns Photography: Ian Wallace, Styling: Michelle Noerianto Tomato & Harissa Soup Photography: Ben Dearnley, Styling: Julz Beresford | Summer Pea Soup with Smoked Trout Salad Photography: Steve Brown, Styling: Michelle Noerianto | Salmorejo Photography: Petrina Tinslay, Styling: Michelle Noerianto

Hot Soups pages 24-31
Thai-style Pumpkin Soup with Coriander Pesto Photography: Mark Roper, Styling: Kristen Anderson | Cauliflower Cheese Soup Photography: Steve Brown, Styling: Michaela Le Compte | Pasta & Fagioli Photography: Ian Wallace, Styling: Julz Beresford | Vietnamese Pho Photography: Ian Wallace, Styling: David Morgan | Easy Fish Chowder Photography: Ben Dearnley, Styling: Michelle Noerianto

Eggs pages 32-39
Egg & Chips Photography: Mark Roper, Styling: Lisa La Barbera | Coddled Eggs with Crunchy Croûtons & Smoked Salmon Photography: Ben Dearnley, Styling: Michelle Noerianto | Asian-style Fried Egg on Bean Sprout Salad Photography: Georgie Cole, Styling: Julz Beresford | The Perfect Herb Omelette Photography: Ian Wallace, Styling: Michelle Noerianto | Spiced Coconut Eggs Photography: Steve Brown, Styling: Julz Beresford

Boiled Pasta pages 40-47
Pasta Puttanesca Photography: Ian Wallace, Styling: Emma Garside | Pasta with Lemon & Goat Cheese Photography: Ben Dearnley, Styling: Jane Hann | Pasta with Pepper Steak Photography: Luke Burgess, Styling: Julz Beresford Spaghetti with Ricotta & Rocket Photography: Ian Wallace, Styling: Louise Pickford | Bucatini with Salsa Verde Photography: Ben Dearnley, Styling: Michelle Noerianto

Baked Pasta pages 48-55
Turkey Macaroni Bake Steve Brown, Styling: Michelle Noerianto | Butternut & Goat Cheese Lasagne Photography: Ian Wallace, Styling: Michelle Noerianto Pasta Stacks Photography: Mark Roper, Styling: Michelle Noerianto | Lamb & Pasta Bake with Roasted Tomatoes Photography: Ian Wallace, Styling: Michelle Noerianto Baked Penne with Roasted Vegetables Photography: Prue Ruscoe, Styling: Michelle Noerianto

Pizzas pages 56-63
Bread Pizzas Photography: Ben Dearnley, Michelle Noerianto | Deli Pizza Photography: Ian Wallace, Styling: Julz Beresford | Potato Pizza Photography: Ian Wallace, Styling: Michelle Noerianto | Wild Mushroom Pizza Photography: Ian Wallace, Styling: Michelle Noerianto | Midweek Pizza Photography: Steve Brown, Styling: Michelle Noerianto

Savoury Tarts pages 64-71
Little Hummus & Herb Salad Tarts Photography: Ian Wallace, Styling: Louise Pickford | Mascarpone & Gorgonzola Tart Photography: Steve Brown, Styling: Michelle Noerianto | Fig & Goat Cheese Tranche Photography: Ian Wallace, Styling: Louise Pickford | Torta Caprese Photography: Ben Dearnley, Styling: Michelle Noerianto | Roasted Vegetable Tart Photography: Ian Wallace, Styling: Louise Pickford

Rice pages 72-79
Smoked Fish Risotto with Poached Eggs Photography: Steve Brown, Styling: Michelle Noerianto | Nasi Goreng Photography: Ben Dearnley, Styling: Michelle Noerianto | Pumpkin & Goat Cheese Risotto Photography: Ben Dearnley, Styling: Julz Beresford | Stir-fried Vegetable Rice Photography: Ian Wallace, Styling: Louise Pickford | Easy Paella Photography: John Paul Urizar, Styling: David Morgan

Vegetarian Mains pages 80-87
Rosemary Veggie Kebabs with Seasoned Rice Photography: William Meppem, Styling: David Morgan | Pea & Haloumi Fritters Photography: Steve Brown, Styling: Kristen Anderson | Lentil & Cauliflower Pilaf Photography: Steve Brown, Styling: Kristen Anderson | Oven-roasted Veggies with Feta Dressing Photography: Ian Wallace, Styling: Louise Pickford | Baked Aubergine with Goat Cheese Photography: Ian Wallace, Styling: Michelle Noerianto

Salads pages 88-95
The New Greek Salad Photography: Ian Wallace, Styling: Michelle Noerianto | Quail Salad with Chinese Marbled Eggs Photography: Ian Wallace, Styling: Michelle Noerianto | Thai Beef Salad Photography: Ian Wallace, Styling: Louise Pickford | Smoked Chicken, Cherry & Avocado Salad Photography: Mark Roper, Styling: Julz Beresford | Crumbed Bocconcini & Roast Tomato Salad Photography: John Paul Urizar, Styling: David Morgan

Potato pages 96-103
Creamy Mashed Potato Photography: Ian Wallace, Styling: Michelle Noerianto | Potato Pancakes with Smoked Salmon Photography: Ian Wallace, Styling: Michelle Noerianto Little Lancashire Hotpots Photography: Ian Wallace, Styling: Michelle Noerianto | Spicy Potatoes with Poppadams Photography: Ian Wallace, Styling: Michelle Noerianto Tartiflette Photography: Mark Roper, Styling: David Morgan

Vegetables pages 104-111
Parmesan Carrots with Aioli Photography: Sam McAdam Styling: Michelle Noerianto | Fennel with Orange & Olives Photography: Mark Roper, Styling: David Morgan | Broad

Beans with Pangrattato Photography: Ian Wallace, Styling: Michelle Noerianto | Chickpeas with Spinach Photography: Ian Wallace, Styling: Michelle Noerianto | Peperonata Photography: Ian Wallace, Styling: Michelle Noerianto

White Fish pages 112-119
Pan-fried Fish with Black-Bean Dressing Photography: Ben Dearnley, Styling: Kristen Anderson | Fish with Asparagus & Herb Vinaigrette Photography: Ian Wallace, Styling: Michelle Noerianto | Fish with Herb & Walnut Crust Photography: Ben Dearnley, Styling: Michelle Noerianto | Fish Provençal Photography: Steve Brown, Styling: Jane Hann | Swordfish with Agrodolce Photography: Ian Wallace, Styling: Julz Beresford

Salmon pages 120-127
Salmon Roulade with Crab Sauce Photography: Ben Dearnley, Styling: Julz Beresford | Glazed Salmon with Lime Beurre Blanc & Tomato, Ginger & Basil Salsa Photography: Ian Wallace, Styling: Michelle Noerianto | Salmon Rillettes with Bagel Toasts Photography: Ben Dearnley, Styling: Julz Beresford | Cajun Salmon with Corn Salsa Photography: Mark Roper, Styling: Julz Beresford | Glazed Salmon with Parsnip Purée Photography: Ian Wallace, Styling: Michelle Noerianto

Chicken pages 128-135
Chicken with Pesto & Mascarpone Photography: Mark Roper, Styling: Deb McLean | Chicken Cacciatore Photography: Ben Dearnley, Styling: Michelle Noerianto | Simple Moroccan Chicken Photography: Steve Brown, Styling: Julz Beresford Minced Chicken with Thai Basil Photography: John Paul Urizar, Styling: David Morgan | Chicken with Peaches & Vanilla Photography: Mark Roper, Styling: Julz Beresford

Pork pages 136-143
Spanish Pork Photography: Ben Dearnley, Styling: Jane Hann | Tuscan Pork with Warm Fig Salsa Photography: Ian Wallace, Styling: Michelle Noerianto | Pork Fillet with Cherry Sauce Photography: Steve Brown, Styling: Kristen Anderson | Rack of Pork with Cider Apples Photography: Emma Reilly, Styling: David Morgan | Pork with Strawberry Balsamic Sauce Photography: Ben Dearnley, Styling: Julz Beresford

Lamb pages 144-151
Lamb Shanks French Daube-Style Photography: Ian Wallace, Styling: Michelle Noerianto | Lamb Stir-fry with Coconut Rice Photography: Steve Brown, Styling: Julz Beresford | Rack of Lamb with Chilli-Mint Sauce Photography: Steve Brown, Styling: Michelle Noerianto Easy Lamb Pilaf Photography: Ben Dearnley, Styling: Jane Hann | Moroccan Lamb with Chickpea Salad Photography: William Meppem, Styling: David Morgan

Beef pages 152-159
Beef with Wild Mushroom Vinaigrette Photography: Mark Roper, Styling: Julz Beresford | Steak & Kidney Tartlets Photography: Steve Brown, Styling: Michelle Noerianto Cubed Steak with Chilli & Coriander Dressing Photography: Petrina Tinslay, Styling: David Morgan | Rare Beef & Horseradish Galette Photography: Steve Brown, Styling: Julz Beresford | Fillet of Beef Bourguignon Photography: Steve Brown, Styling: Michelle Noerianto

Stir-fries pages 160-167
Stir-fried Noodles with Beef & Greens Photography: Petrina Tinslay, Styling: Michelle Noerianto | Spicy Stir-fried Aubergine Photography: Steve Brown, Styling: Michelle Noerianto | Stir-fried Rice with Chilli Tuna Photography: Ian Wallace, Styling: Michelle Noerianto | Thai-style Pork & Hokkien Noodle Stir-fry Photography: Steve Brown, Styling: Michelle Noerianto | Stir-fry Chicken with Pesto Photography: Luke Burgess, Styling: Julz Beresford

Casseroles pages 168-175
Fruity Beef Casserole Photography: Jared Fowler, Styling: Michelle Noerianto | Venison Casserole Photography: Steve Brown, Styling: Michelle Noerianto | Polenta with Sausage Casserole Photography: Ian Wallace, Styling: Michelle Noerianto | Chorizo & Bean Stew Photography: Steve Brown, Styling: Michelle Noerianto | Lamb Tagine Photography: Ben Dearnley, Styling: Michelle Noerianto

Curries pages 176-183
Thai Chicken & Asparagus Curry Photography: Ben Dearnley, Styling: David Morgan | Low-fat Kofta Curry Photography: Steve Brown, Styling: Michaela Le Compte | Lamb & Aubergine Curry Photography: Ian Wallace, Styling: Michelle Noerianto | Easy Masaman Curry Photography: Ian Wallace, Styling: Michelle Noerianto | Coconut & Chicken Curry Photography: Georgie Cole, Styling: Michelle Noerianto

Sweet Tarts & Pies pages 184-191
Little Pear Tartlets Photography: Ben Dearnley, Styling: Michelle Noerianto | Mascarpone & Cherry Tarts Photography: Ian Wallace, Styling: Louise Pickford Strawberry Amaretti Tarts Photography: Petrina Tinslay, Styling: Michelle Noerianto | Tarte Tatin Photography: Geoff Lung, Styling: Kristen Anderson | Pear & Ginger Tart Photography: Mark Roper, Styling: Louise Pickford

Cold Desserts pages 192-199
Buttermilk Puddings with Candied Kumquats Photography: Ian Wallace, Styling: Michelle Noerianto Cassata Trifle Photography: Petrina Tinslay, Styling Kristen Anderson | Eton Mess Photography: Ian Wallace, Stylist: Michelle Noerianto | Yoghurt & Berry Brulée Photography: Steve Brown, Styling: Michelle Noerianto Little Pavs with Tropical Fruits & Passion-fruit Sauce Photography: Steve Brown, Styling: Michelle Noerianto

Cheesecakes pages 200-207
White Chocolate Cheesecakes with Mango & Strawberries Photography: Steve Brown, Styling: Michelle Noerianto Banoffee Cheesecake Photography: Geoff Lung, Styling: Michelle Noerianto | New York Cheesecake Photography: Geoff Lung, Styling: Michelle Noerianto | Lemon Lime & Ginger Cheesecakes Photography: Geoff Lung, Styling: Michelle Noerianto | Rosewater Cheesecake Photography: Ben Dearnley, Styling: Julz Beresford

Ice-cream & Semifreddo pages 208-215
Vanilla Gelato with Vanilla Strawberry Sauce Photography: Ben Dearnley, Styling: Michelle Noerianto Nougat Semifreddo with Blueberry Compote Photography: Ian Wallace, Styling: Michelle Noerianto | Baci Ice-cream

Photography: Ian Wallace, Styling: Louise Pickford | Iced Raspberry Parfait Photography: Geoff Lung, Styling: Michelle Noerianto | Lemon & Mascarpone Sorbetto Photography: Mark Roper, Styling: Kristen Anderson

Hot Puddings pages 216-223

Raspberry & White Chocolate Waffle Pudding Photography: Ben Dearnley, Styling: Michelle Noerianto | Caramel Apple Pudding Photography Mark Roper, Styling: Julz Beresford Warm Brownie Puddings with Chocolate Sauce Photography: Petrina Tinslay, Styling: Kristen Anderson Malted Chocolate Pudding with Mars Bar Custard Photography: Ian Wallace, Styling: Michelle Noerianto Orange Bread & Butter Pudding Photography: Ben Dearnley, Styling: Michelle Noerianto

Pikelets & Pancakes pages 224-231

Blueberry Pancakes with Mango Butter & Cream Photography: Ben Dearnley, Styling: Steve Brown, Michelle Noerianto | Blintz with Sour Cream & Cherries Photography: Ian Wallace, Styling Julz Beresford | Orange Hotcakes Photography: Ian Wallace, Styling: Emma Garside | Coconut Pancakes with Palm Sugar Syrup Photography: Ian Wallace, Styling: Julz Beresford | Crêpes with Walnut Cream & Butterscotch Sauce Photography: Ian Wallace, Styling: Julz Beresford

Big Cakes pages 232-239

Chocolate Cherry Liqueur Cake Photography: Geoff Lung, Styling: Michelle Noerianto | Strawberry Vacherin Photography: Ben Dearnley, Styling: Michelle Noerianto | Semolina Shortbread with Caramelized Apples Photography: Petrina Tinslay, Styling: Michelle Noerianto | Plum Cake with Plum Syrup Photography: Petrina Tinslay, Styling: Michelle Noerianto | Orange Syrup Cake Photography: Ian Wallace, Styling: Emma Garside

Small Cakes pages 240-247

Carrot Cakes Photography: Petrina Tinslay, Styling: Michelle Noerianto | Mini Chocolate Cakes Photography: Mark Roper, Styling: Amber Keller | Lemon Friands with Lemon Curd & Blueberries Photography: Ben Dearnley, Styling: Michelle Noerianto | Strawberry Lamingtons Photography: Steve Brown, Styling: Michelle Noerianto **Mini Gingerbreads** Photography: Petrina Tinslay, Styling: Jane Hann

Thanks, too, for assistance with recipe development on the following: to Sally James, whose *Escape to Yountville* inspired Prosciutto Wraps, (page 9); to Lisa La Barbera, for Egg & Chips (page 33); and to Nancy Duran, for Deli Pizza (page 58).

A success story like *delicious.* is not possible without the diverse talents of many people. Firstly, there are the wonderful celebrity chefs whose recipes and stories are so much part of the magazine; our CEO Michael McHugh, who turned the dream into a reality and who, with the very talented Neale Whitaker, came up with our regular features including 'Wicked', 'Tuesday Night Cooking' and 'Seasonal Flavours'; our editor-in-chief, Trudi Jenkins, whose vision keeps the magazine ever-evolving, and of course all the editorial staff and the food teams past and present who couldn't help but get caught up in the passion that captured us all. And naturally we couldn't have done it without the unique band of photographers and stylists whose creative talent helps set the magazine apart from the rest, or our friends at the ABC, who constantly offer enthusiastic and invaluable support for the magazine and, particularly, this book. Finally, a very special thanks to our publishing team at Quadrille – Alison, Jane and Claire. It's not easy compiling a book when 12,000 miles separate you, but you have managed to create something very special of which we can all be proud.